THE KIDS' BOOK ABOUT DEATH AND DYING

BY AND FOR KIDS

THE KIDS' BOOK ABOUT DEATH AND DYING

BY AND FOR KIDS

The Unit at Fayerweather Street School
Edited and Coordinated by
Eric E. Rofes

LITTLE, BROWN AND COMPANY
Boston   Toronto

FIRST EDITION

Library of Congress Cataloging in Publication Data
Main entry under title:
The Kids' book about death and dying.

   Summary: Fourteen children offer facts and advice
to give young readers a better understanding of death.
   1. Children and death—Juvenile literature.
2. Death—Juvenile literature.   3. Death—Psychological
aspects—Juvenile literature.   [1. Death.
2. Children's writings]
I. Rofes, Eric E., 1954–   . II. Fayerweather Street
School. Unit.
BF723.D3K53   1985   155.9'37   85-180
ISBN 0-316-75390-4

BP

DESIGNED BY JEANNE F. ABBOUD

*Published simultaneously in Canada
by Little, Brown & Company (Canada) Limited*

PRINTED IN THE UNITED STATES OF AMERICA

To
the Memory
of

WILLY DOG
(1968–1982)

Contents

Acknowledgments

We would like to acknowledge the help of the following people who contributed to our understanding of the topic of death and dying: Barbara Hayes Buell, Esq., Judy Grant, Debby Alexander, Dorothy Meyer, Elizabeth Abbe, Annie Fisher, Jorie Hunken, Pat Sargent, S. Norman Sherry, M.D., Nathan Albert, Rabbi Earl Grollman, Charles Keefe, Nat Stoddard, Juliet Hills, Peter Richards, Katey Hickey, Dr. Yashar Bahceli, Mindy Sobota, the Colenback family, Lisa Marlin, Carol Hamilton, C. G. Hori, M.D., Linda Brown, Kay McClain, Deirdre Leopold, Ellen Mass, Helene Stern, Huck Gintis, Karen Glantz, Fern Fisher, Joy Natoli and the Samaritans of Boston, Rosemary Whiting and Earl Meyers. We want to thank the late Norma Farber for helping us to understand the aging process and we'd like to thank Geri Schumacher, R.N., for all her help throughout this long project. We'd also like to thank other children in our school, our parents, and the staff of Fayerweather Street School for their assistance and their support. Linda Brown and Martha Older lent important assistance to us in typing and copying various manuscripts for this book.

We'd like to thank Gerald G. Jampolsky, M.D. for permission to quote from *There is a Rainbow Behind Every Dark Cloud*, The Center for Attitudinal Healing, 1978 (Celestial Arts, Milbrae, CA) and *Straight from the Siblings: Another Look at the Rainbow*, edited by Gloria Murray and Gerald G. Jampolsky, M.D., 1982 (Celestial Arts, Milbrae, CA).

THE KIDS' BOOK ABOUT DEATH AND DYING

BY AND FOR KIDS

Introduction:
How We Wrote This Book

THIS book is made up of the thoughts, percep-
tions, and feelings of fourteen kids between
the ages of eleven and fourteen, members of a class
I worked with called "The Unit" at the Fayerweather Street School in Cambridge, Massachusetts. Although these fourteen individuals are the
core group of authors, many other children in this
open-classroom, independent school have contributed to the book, as have teachers and parents.
While the text primarily reflects the students' attitudes and experiences, the book also includes the
experiences of many others from the school community.

Our class came to write this book on death and
dying in an unusual way. One of my students had
an experience in his family which was very difficult
to handle. His father had a life-threatening disease,
and his doctor was sure that he would not live for

more than a year. When his parents spoke to me about their situation, I had very mixed feelings. I realized that I had never really thought about how to deal with the subject of death and dying with children, and I didn't know very much about the subject. I decided that it would be interesting and beneficial for all of us to learn about death and dying.

Although many people assume that kids have no experience with death, all of us have had some connection with death in our lives. Alex, for instance, had experienced the death of his two pet mice, and this had made him think about death and dying and raised some questions in his mind. Jamey was very much affected by her grandfather's death, which occurred shortly after we started work on this book. Some of the other kids in the Unit had experienced the death of a parent, a sibling, or the deaths of other close relatives.

We formed an informal discussion group in September 1981. No one was required to participate in the project. We soon saw that talking about death affected us in different ways. Seth, at times, felt sad, because our talks made him recall experiences that he didn't really want to remember. Billy felt a bit awkward and strange when death was discussed, because he didn't have a clear idea of exactly what it was. He said, "It's like talking about a television show you've never watched."

Participating in a large discussion group helped the kids avoid becoming depressed by the subject of death. They received constant feedback and support from each other, as they raised questions and offered answers. Many of the kids, for example, found that they had the same reaction to hearing about a person dying. As Macy put it, "I don't really feel sad unless I actually knew the person well. Instead I feel very nervous, and my knees go to mush and butterflies start fluttering around my stomach." Many of the kids shared this nervousness.

In addition to our discussions, we came up with various exercises and projects to help us understand our feelings, including dramatic improvisations. As a group, we read many articles, pamphlets, and books — including *Death Be Not Proud*, *Brian's Song*, and *Jonathan Livingston Seagull*. We also watched movies, television shows, and videotapes on the subject. The kids also did some drawing and writing, most of it focused on their personal experiences with death and dying.

In January the students began interviewing other children, parents, and other adults on this topic and tape-recording their conversations. They talked to kids of all ages who had different experiences and perspectives than they had, and adults who worked in suicide-prevention services, hospices (places that dying people visit to get support and help), and hospitals. They talked to doctors, nurses, veterinarians, lawyers, rabbis, priests, funeral directors, and cemetery workers. They visited health centers, clinics, hospitals, funeral homes, and graveyards. We gathered all this information together and developed our own perspective on various aspects of death and dying.

After the interviews, the kids transcribed the tapes, copying down — sometimes word for word — the text of each interview. Then each student picked a major topic area to write about. These included "Medical Aspects of Death and Dying," "Death of Pets," "Death of Children," "Funeral Customs" and "Supernatural, Reincarnation, and Immortality." Some of these topics, which later became chapters for the book, were written by individual children, and others were written by two or three together. Their own stories and thoughts were added to the information they had culled. Then the author(s) of each chapter would read it aloud to the other kids in the core group to get their feedback.

The text of the book was finished by early spring. At this time, various people in Fayerweather Street School helped us by typing the manuscript, correcting it, and making suggestions about ways it could be improved. We then presented it to our editors at Little, Brown. Then the process of printing and publicizing the book began.

We believe that children deserve to have straightforward answers to their questions about death and dying, and we hope that this book provides helpful information to children. We also hope that this book will be useful to parents and people who work with children, who are curious about the ways in which kids experience death and dying. By providing the thoughts and feelings of children who have spent a year studying this subject, we hope that more people will find the courage to talk openly and candidly with children about this important topic.

— Eric E. Rofes

with

Seth Boyd	Alex Lockwood
Caleb Brown	Kama Lurie
Elizabeth Carr	Stephen Lynch
Jamey Chancey-O'Quinn	John McClain
Joy Koller	Susanna Steele
Macy Lawrence	Tanya Wasserman
Kate Leopold	Billy Yokoyama

⫷1⫸

Learning to Talk About Death

EVERYBODY alive today will die eventually. This includes you and me and all of us. "Everybody is mortal," Dr. Norman Sherry, Caleb's doctor, said, when we talked to him. "So we are all expected to die, although we don't always admit that to ourselves. But when we think about it, we all expect to die sometime. Most of us expect this to happen when we are old. Everyone expects their parents to die some time and, because this is usually very painful to face, you don't think about it a lot. Even older people hate to think about their parents dying. We are always children in the eyes of our mothers and fathers, and we never expect our children to die."

Because people don't want to face the reality of death, they rarely talk about it. "Talking about death is like talking about sex — people don't talk about it until they have to," Elizabeth said. It is clear that society, in general, fears dying. People fear death because they don't know what it is. They understand life and know what it is all about, but they don't know anything about death. They don't know what's going to happen after they die. Is there some sort of afterlife? If heaven and hell do exist, which one will they go to?

Many adults fear death because of the way they were brought up. If people are taught that death is mysterious or something to be afraid of, then that's what they'll tell their kids. And so this attitude is passed down through the generations.

Adults may not want to discuss death with their kids because they want to protect them from unnecessary pain, and because they themselves know how it hurts. They also may think that children aren't experienced or old enough to understand death.

Sometimes, because adults can't be direct about dying, they lie about death or cover it up to make it easier for kids to deal with. When Caleb's mother, Linda Brown, was a little girl, her mother ran over their cat while they were leaving the driveway. When Linda came home she was told the cat had had stomach trouble and was in the hospital, even though it was still flattened on the driveway.

Other times adults may try to butter up a child by doing something fun, like going to the movies or for ice cream, and, after the child is in a good mood, they tell the bad news. They think that because they've done all these fun things, the child won't mind the death as much. Sometimes an adult lets the child bring up the subject because he or she doesn't know how to tell the child.

Some adults try to make death sound attractive by saying things like, "Dear, your uncle has passed on," rather than saying "Your uncle is dead." Other such phrases are: "passed away"; "gone to sleep"; "won't be with us"; "joined their ancestors"; "met his Maker." At Macy's great-aunt's funeral, the priest said, "Now, friends, Margaret has now crossed the holy bridge of life — isn't that wonderful!" Macy says, "I would rather be going out to dinner or to the beach than crossing the holy bridge of life. I think the priest used these words to comfort people so they would think that Margaret was happy now."

Our preference is for children to be told straight out that someone has died — using the word "died" or "death." This is frank, and to the point.

Because many parents don't know how to teach their children about death, some children first learn about death from television, radio, and movies. In television cartoons, death seems not to be important — instead it's funny. People are shot and then in the next scene they're okay, or the Coyote will have boulders dropped on him or fall off a canyon, and he'll just walk away with a perturbed look on his face and go after the Roadrunner again. Some movies and television shows treat death as it really is, but others are overly gory and very unrealistic. The characters almost never die of old age; they die of extraordinary causes — terrible chemical exposure, or invaders from outer space, for instance. These shows and movies give the impression that death is scary, gruesome, violent, and undignified.

News media — television, newspapers, and magazines — can also give kids false impressions about death. When Macy was four, she would watch the morning news on television and see large numbers of people killed in Vietnam or in planes that crashed. She'd go to her mother and say, "Seventy-eight people were killed yesterday." She didn't know what she was talking about, but she was interested because of the big numbers. Her mother, who would usually be asleep at this early time in the morning, would just roll over and say, "That's nice, Macy," and go back to sleep. The problem with many television news shows is that they tell you about death without showing any emotions. This makes death seem unreal and impersonal.

In addition, the facts presented to us on television and radio and in newspapers and magazines may not always be correct. When an important figure in politics or entertainment dies, for example, reporters rush to the scene to get the news before anyone else does, or before their paper goes to press, and often they can't wait around until all of the facts surrounding the death have been uncovered.

So the public may hear only part of the story at first, and the facts may change many times in a matter of hours. (This happened a few years ago when John Hinckley attempted to assassinate President Reagan.) Some newspapers and magazines try to attract readers with sensational stories about celebrities, and if a famous person dies, they may not stick to the truth, but instead may try to lead their readers into thinking that the person died under suspicious circumstances. This is all very confusing to children and can sometimes make the death of a well-loved public figure even more shocking and traumatic to them.

Even fairy tales can be very violent, and they can lead kids to think that there are an awful lot of people out there just waiting to kill them. "Hansel and Gretel" is a story that used to terrify Macy, because she imagined how it could be adapted to modern-day urban life. A kid could be lured into a car with candy and driven off by someone who would do obscene things to him (instead of shoving him into an oven and cooking and eating him). Fairy tales can also be misleading because they stretch the truth — dead people are brought back to life through spells, for instance. This may make little kids think that they are safe from death.

Death should be talked about clearly and honestly, so that it can be understood by kids. Death should be dealt with in schools. Discussion groups, in which students can talk to each other about their various experiences with death, can comfort as well as teach children. Even the death of a classroom pet can become easier to accept if the whole class is able to help each other and talk about it and learn together.

Kids can also learn about death by reading good nonfiction books that give complete information, or by reading good fiction, such as *White Fang* or *Ordinary People,* which can give a child a clearer idea about death before it happens to him or someone close to him.

If a child is brought up in a family in which the members talk about death and are open about it, then the child gets a better understanding of what death is and won't be as afraid of it. Adults have experienced having people close to them die, usually more than kids have, and therefore, they know some things that kids don't know. Also, adults often have more information about the specifics of burial, cremation, gravestones, and funerals. These subjects are a mystery to most kids.

Susanna's family has always been open about talking about death. "When I was little," Susanna remembers, "my sister and I talked about life after death and decided which animals we'd like to come back as. My mother would talk about death when pets died. This helped me a lot. If my family wasn't open about death, I think I might believe it wasn't going to happen to me or that it is a very scary thing."

Kids who are brought up in families able to talk about death understand it better. Susanna thinks that her two-year-old brother Miguel knows a lot more about what death means than most other children his age. When their cat, Max, was recently killed, their mother talked to them and explained death. Their stepfather buried Max in the backyard, and Miguel was present at the burial. A few days later, Miguel ran up to Susanna and said, "Max is dead. It's very sad, but it's okay."

Joy worked with kids who are four, five, and six years old, and she noticed that some of the children think that dying is just like birth and is therefore a happy thing. Or if they are told by adults that a person who died has gone to heaven, they're happy. Young kids tend to worry about whether they will ever see the dead person again, and parents sometimes tell kids they will see the person when they themselves go to heaven.

When the Unit first started working on the subject of death and dying, each student wrote a paper about his or her earliest experience with death. Some kids had a hard time remembering their first encounter with death, so we did some creative writing exercises to help them remember. Others were surprised at how much their reactions had changed as they grew older.

Jamey: "When I was six or seven I went to visit my great-grandmother. She had a cookie jar with flowers and fruit painted on it. I said it was pretty and that I liked it. My great-grandmother told me, in a low voice, that when she passed away, she would give me the cookie jar. It surprised me, because we'd never talked about death before, and I hadn't really ever thought about someone close to me dying."

Joy had a similar experience with her great-grandmother Lily:

"I was looking through Lily's jewelry and I saw some pieces that interested me, and I said that I'd like to have them. My great-grandmother said, with a smile, 'You can have them all after I die.' I then said to myself with a smile, 'You're never going to die, so I'll never have the jewelry.' A few weeks later, my mother informed me that Lily had died. It shocked me because she'd seemed so healthy just a little while ago. I got a piece of the jewelry, and whenever I see it, it reminds me of what happened."

Caleb: "I used to have a gerbil who died of some disease. I remember the tombstone and decorations part of the dying being more important to me than the death itself."

Macy: "When I was five, my great-grandfather died and I went to the wake. This was the first real sort of death in my family that I can recall. I took great delight in attending the wake because it made me feel very important, and I was also interested to see what a dead person looked like. I never really talked to my great-grandfather so I wasn't really upset, nor did I cry. But I remember my mother was kind of upset and so was my aunt, but by the time we left, my mother and my aunt were actually *joking*, which I thought was sort of dumb, because originally they had gone there to mourn and they came out joking.

"My grandfather got cancer when I was eight and six months later he died. This did not come as a shock to me because it was quite obvious he was going to die. He was my mother's father. She took it sort of bad because both her parents were now dead. I didn't cry at my grandfather's funeral, but I did feel kind of bad.

"I couldn't stand my grandfather's wake; it was worse than the funeral. Everybody said how good and peaceful he looked displayed out there in his coffin. I think that's disgusting, because nobody looks really great when they're dead. I thought my grandfather looked pretty bad, in fact. I remember this chain twisted around his fingers with a cross on it and the way the people made his face up — he looked like a peach. When I die there's no way I'm going to have a wake and have people say how peaceful I look."

Billy: "I could hear my brother talking to me. I could hear my mom crying. Suddenly I felt a dull pain of cold or wind rush over my heart. I got up, ignoring the fact that I was tired and that it was about two in the morning. I rushed downstairs and found my mother lying on the couch in her gown, crying and talking on the telephone. I felt sorry for my mom, but I was too sleepy to stick around, and so I went to bed. When I woke up in the morning, my brother explained to me that Gramma died. I didn't really understand, but I guess I just did my fair share of crying."

We also talked about the way we think death would look if it were a person or an animal. This was interesting, because it helped us to understand our attitudes toward death. We also drew and painted pictures of how we imagine death to look.

Susanna pictures death as an old person who can't walk well without a cane. Death has a wrinkly face and is very short and feels scared. Macy pictures death as a female who is peaceful. She wears white clothing, and has a powder-white face, with a fairly serious expression on it.

When Alex was about four or five, he was scared of dark objects in his room after his mother turned out the lights. He pictured death as a dark skeleton in his room — mainly a bony skull — which was scary. This happened for about two years, and then he got over it.

When Macy was little, she watched a television program called "Rudolf the Red-Nosed Reindeer," and there was an abominable snowman in it — all furry and white with big claws. She pictured death like this. She was afraid that he'd come and carry her away at night, so she left her bedroom door open so the light would come streaming in. She stopped feeling this way about death at age seven, and for a while she didn't think much about what death was like.

When Joy was little, she thought death was a wolf. Her mother had hung up a poster of Little Red Riding Hood and the wolf. When she turned off the lights at night, it looked as if the wolf was going to come out of the poster and attack her. So she demanded that her mother take it down, because it was too scary.

We can think of some times when death is not really so bad. If a cat is very sick and suffering, and you have a choice of helping it to die a quick, painless death or letting it live, helping the cat die by taking it to a vet for a fatal injection would be best, to end its suffering. Similarly, if a person is really sick and/or suffering, it might be a relief to him or her to die, because it puts an end to the misery.

Also, if you're very old and feeble, and living is a constant struggle, you might feel ready to die.

Some deaths, however, we find to be particularly tragic. We are very sad when someone is healthy and then in a fatal accident. Also, deaths that occur as a result of war are a waste of human life. It is tragic when babies die, because they haven't had a chance to see what the world is like, and they haven't had time to do anything yet.

No matter how a person dies, however, death is an inevitable, natural part of life. And it is important to examine our feelings about death so that we can come to accept it without fear. But, along with our feelings, we should be aware of the medical facts about death — what it is, what causes it, and what happens when we die.

☙ 2 ❧

What Is Death?

RIGHT now someone is dying. Actually, many people are dying all over the world. About every nineteen seconds a person dies somewhere.

People die from all kinds of causes. Some diseases kill only adults, some only children. For kids, the death rate has been going down for a long time. Fewer children are dying from infectious diseases, such as smallpox and polio, than in the past. Years ago, when someone got pneumonia, for example, about all the doctor could do was cross his fingers and sit with the person. Some people even died from colds. There weren't any vaccinations against malaria or polio, so that in most cases when you caught those diseases, that was it for you.

Though today most cases of pneumonia can be treated with a little penicillin, there are still many diseases that have no cure. Brain tumors and cancer are among them. We read *Death Be Not Proud,* about a teenager who had a brain tumor and tried all the possibilities available at the time, including injections of mustard, a special diet, and surgery. These methods seemed to work at first, but in the end they were all in vain. Some diseases are still a mystery.

On page 22 is a list of the top causes of adult death today. We found them listed in *Ca — A Cancer Journal for Clinicians,* published by the American Cancer Society (Jan./Feb. 1981, Vol. 31, No. 1).

WHAT ARE SOME OF THESE DISEASES?

The number-one cause of death is *diseases of the heart* — primarily heart attacks. A heart attack occurs when part of the heart muscle is damaged and is unable to pump enough blood to keep a person alive.

Cancers are caused when abnormal, or *malignant,* cells in a person grow too fast and kill off normal cells. Some types of cancer can be cured through various kinds of treatment.

Cerebrovascular diseases interrupt the blood supply to the brain, thereby damaging part of it. They are also called strokes or severe shock.

Influenza is commonly called the flu. The flu is a disease that in a healthy person causes headaches, body aches, and fever, and other cold-like symp-

RANK	CAUSE OF DEATH	NUMBER OF DEATHS	DEATH RATE PER 100,000 POP.	PERCENT OF TOTAL DEATH
	All Causes	1,899,597	816.3	100 %
1	*Diseases of Heart*	718,850	303.4	37.8%
2	*Cancers*	386,686	168.4	20.4%
3	*Cerebrovascular Disease*	181,934	75.3	9.6%
4	*Accidents*	103,202	45.4	5.4%
5	*Influenza and Pneumonia*	51,193	21.4	2.7%
6	*Diabetes Mellitus*	32,984	14.1	1.7%
7	*Cirrhosis of Liver*	30,848	14	1.6%
8	*Arteriosclerosis*	28,754	12	1.5%
9	*Suicide*	28,681	12.6	1.5%
10	*Diseases of Infancy*	23,401	13	1.2%
11	*Homicide*	19,968	8.6	1.1%
12	*Emphysema*	16,376	7.1	0.9%
13	*Congenital Anomalies*	12,983	6.3	0.7%
14	*Nephritis and Neprosis*	8,519	3.7	0.5%
15	*Septicemia and Pyemia*	7,112	3.2	0.4%
	Other and Ill-Defined	248,101	107.3	13.1%

Age-adjusted to the 1970 U.S. Census Population. Source: National Center for Health Statistics.

toms. In old and/or unhealthy people, this infection can overload their systems and kill them. *Pneumonia* is an infection of the lungs.

These top four diseases, along with accidents, account for a little over seventy-five percent of all human deaths.

Various diseases take different amounts of time to kill people. A heart attack may kill a person instantly, for example, while some forms of cancer may linger for years before they prove fatal.

Some diseases run in families, meaning they *may* be passed down from generation to generation. If your grandparents and parents experience a disease, you might also. Some of these hereditary diseases include cancer, high blood pressure, birth defects, and diabetes.

But what exactly *is* death? How can we tell when someone is dead?

John's mother, Kay McClain, who is a nurse, was in the emergency room of the hospital in which she works when a baby with a brain tumor was brought in. She told us: "The child had a brain tumor and had a deformity of the head, and it looked very sickly. It wasn't the normal size for a child, and the child's color was bad. It had been undergoing, evidently, a lot of treatment in the past. This was a very difficult situation. . . ."

When cases like this arrive in hospitals, and death occurs while the doctor or nurse is present, the hospital must legally confirm that the patient has died so they don't get into legal trouble. They confirm the death by monitoring the heartbeat and the breathing. When the person has died, the heartbeat and the breathing stop. The doctor then records the time and the cause of death.

But people are now questioning whether this is sufficient proof of death.

WHEN IS SOMEONE LEGALLY DEAD?

At present, the accepted definition of death is the moment when a person stops breathing and his or her heart stops beating. Cells — the tiny, microscopic units that make up our bodies — require an oxygen supply in order to live and reproduce. When a person's heart and breathing stop, the oxygen supply is cut off and the cells begin to die. The first kind of cells that begin to die, once a person has stopped breathing, are the brain cells. They start dying in about three to six minutes after the oxygen flow has been cut off.

Although this definition sounds straightforward, there are problems with it. The main difficulty is that, because doctors are now able to keep a person alive with respiratory machines that control his or her breathing and heartbeat, the person's body itself is not responsible for keeping life going. Often the body is functioning but the brain has died. Should a body in this condition be considered alive or dead?

Sustaining life in this way also raises many moral questions, such as the question of *euthanasia.*

EUTHANASIA

Euthanasia is, according to the American Heritage School Dictionary (1972): "the act of killing a person thought to be incurably ill or injured, in order to spare him suffering." *Passive euthanasia* involves the discontinuing of treatment, and/or turning off machines that keep a person alive. *Active euthanasia* means giving a lethal dose of a drug to a person.

Some people think that euthanasia is out-and-out murder. Others think it has some positive points that should be considered. For instance, if someone is in great pain, or is doomed to live out an inactive, "vegetable" existence and is being kept alive only by machines, he or she might want to die. Keeping someone alive through machines presents many problems, such as the emotional conflict experienced by the family, the uncertain amount of time that "life" can be sustained in this way, and the money it costs to run these machines. The dignity of the dying person also has to be considered.

Caleb wrote this about euthanasia:

"I think that people should legally be able to choose when and under what conditions they die. Since people choose and make decisions in life, why not about their death? If the person is somehow unable to make the decision, then I think that the parents and friends should be included and act as a large decision-making body for the person. If it is a baby that the doctor believes is going to be unable to live normally, then the doctor should definitely consult and talk with the parents before making any decision."

Many people opposed to this kind of euthanasia believe that God controls when people die, and that they should bear with the suffering and the pain until death comes. One of the complicating aspects of this is that miracles can and do happen, and a person who is very sick and suffering can heal and live a good life. Unfortunately, sickness is never predictable.

The concept of "brain death" originated with researchers at the Harvard Medical School in Boston, Massachusetts, about fifteen years ago. The human brain, when alive, always is sending out small electric impulses, even during deep comas (a coma is a state of deep unconsciousness that can be mistaken for death). Since the brain does not send out these impulses when it is dead, if you monitor the impulses and none are coming out, and there is no movement in the body, or it's not breathing on its own, and the patient does not seem to feel and see anything, and has no reflexes, then brain death may have occurred. If these tests are repeated twenty-four hours later, and the same results occur, and there is no evidence of unusually low fever or drug intoxication, then the person has experienced brain death.*

Doctors determine brain death by placing electrodes on the person's scalp to pick up any impulses sent out by the brain. The impulses are amplified one million times by an EKG machine and recorded on a moving strip of paper by an electromagnetic pen. The brain waves of a healthy person are usually curving waves, like a slinky. If the line is flat, or straight, brain death is said to have occurred.

The brain death definition has its problems, too. Currently it is not considered a legal definition of death in all states. Another problem concerns people having "lived" as long as four weeks without significant detected electrical activity in their brain: should they be considered dead? Some scientists who believe in using brain death as a legal definition, feel that the electrical activity cannot be monitored accurately enough through present techniques, such as electrodes. So using brain death as a definition of human death is not perfect, either.

*John Langone, *Death Is a Noun: A View of the End of Life* (Boston: Little, Brown and Company, 1972), pp. 57–82.

CERTIFYING THE DEATH

A complicated procedure is used to certify that a person is actually dead. This procedure varies from state to state.

In one hospital we visited, the physician who originally declares the person dead has to fill out questions on a death certificate, such as name and address. Next, a medical examiner fills in the cause and time of death. Later, a mortician or a funeral director may check off some additional general information. The original certificate is finally taken to the security area in the hospital, where a copy is made and stored.

If there is some dispute about whether the person is actually dead or not, measures are taken to double-check with special machines that monitor brain waves. Some doctors say this is more reliable than simply declaring the body dead when its breathing stops.

AUTOPSIES AND WHAT THEY ARE

"Autopsies are the most scientific way of determining the cause of death," according to Dr. George Hori, a forensic pathologist serving the Arlington-Belmont-Cambridge area near our school. Autopsies are careful medical studies used to find out exactly what caused a person's death. Not everyone who dies has an autopsy. The state has the right to ask for an autopsy to be performed when someone dies under certain circumstances that might be suspicious, involving such causes as violence, injuries at their workplace, malnutrition, drugs, or sexual abuse, or when a person dies suddenly and without obvious cause, or is simply found dead.

If someone dies under any of these conditions, doctors perform an autopsy. Before the doctors can do so, they must get permission from the next of kin (the closest relative of the dead person). If the family does not want an autopsy to be performed, they may be able to refuse permission or put a restriction of some kind on the autopsy. For instance, the family may say that the medical examiner or pathologist cannot take out and examine the heart.

Once permission for the autopsy is given, the medical examiner or pathologist examines the surface and internal organs of the body and tries to figure out the cause of death. If the body is dangerous because the person had large doses of radiation for cancer, or the person had an infectious disease, the medical examiner or pathologist will take the proper precautions, and tell the mortician to do the same. After the medical examiner or pathologist is done, he or she replaces all the organs, and sews the body up. Then the body is buried (or is disposed of in whatever way the family plans).

AFTER DEATH HAS OCCURRED . . .

After a death occurs in a hospital or at home, and the death certificate has been made out, one of several things can happen to the body. It may be transported to a funeral home to be prepared for burial at a cemetery. Or the corpse may be taken to a place called a crematorium and burned to ashes, which are then handed over to the designated surviving relative or friend.

There are still other alternatives. An individual may decide to donate his or her body for scientific research. Or, if you are wealthy enough, you can even try to avoid death by having your body frozen. When a person is still alive, he or she can sign a contract and pay about $75,000 to be frozen from the moment of death until sometime in the future. Unfortunately, at this time no one can guarantee that once a body is thawed it can be revived!*

We will take a closer look at more conventional funeral customs in the next chapter.

*Peter Beardsley, "The Selling of Immortality through Freezing," *Northwest Magazine*, Sunday Oregonian (Portland, Oregon), September 2, 1979.

❧ 3 ❧

Funeral Customs

THE FUNERAL DIRECTOR

WHEN a person dies and his or her surviving family and/or friends want to hold a funeral, they usually consult a mortician or funeral director. The funeral director works with the family and friends of the dead person to make the arrangements for the funeral or memorial service. Funeral directors also sell caskets, the box-like containers in which bodies are buried.

Many people think this must be a depressing and disgusting job to have. We were curious about it, so a few of us went to a funeral home near our school and spoke to Charles Keefe, who has been a funeral director for ten years. He old us: "I find satisfaction in the work I do." We talked to him about his job and about funeral work in general, and we asked him why he chose to pursue this kind of work. Mr.

Keefe said, "The reason I am in the funeral business is because I believe that wakes and funerals can be helpful and comforting for people. Say that one of your parents died, particularly if they died suddenly and you had them cremated right away. Studies have shown that people go through a process where they actually deny that the person has died because they have never actually seen them dead. If the person had been sick, they may have seen death coming on, but a sudden death is different. That is the whole purpose of having a wake at a funeral home. It gives people a place to feel their grief—they come in, talk to the family, witness the death. They understand what has happened and they accept that a friend or loved person is dead."

Mr. Keefe also told us the difference between a wake and a memorial service. A memorial service is when people get together to remember the person who has died. They might sing songs, make speeches, and discuss the deceased. The body is not present at the memorial service. A wake is similar, but the body is present, and people have the opportunity to see it. A wake helps people accept the fact that a person has died and is not coming back.

One part of Mr. Keefe's job is doing the embalming work. Embalming involves injecting a fluid into the arteries to replace the blood. This is done to clean and disinfect the corpse and slow down the decomposing process. This way a body can be available at the wake or the funeral for people to see. Mr. Keefe told us: "Embalming is the preservation of the body and is a very important part of the funeral process. We use cosmetics to try to make the person look at rest and peaceful. It can be soothing to the family if they can see their loved one looking restful, especially if the person had gone through a long illness. It assures them that the pain is finally over."

We learned a lot from Mr. Keefe about embalming procedures. He also showed us around the funeral home. We saw the two rooms where the wakes take place, and the small room where people go to select the casket they want. There are many different kinds to choose from. Caskets may be cheap or expensive. A cheap one might be made of thin metal or pine wood and have cloth pillows, wooden handles, and be very plain. An expensive one might have gold handles and silk pillows and be made of solid cherry wood.

We also asked Mr. Keefe about the costs of funerals. He told us, "Funerals can vary in price from four hundred to twenty-five hundred dollars. Usually if a family chooses to have a memorial service and cremation, it only costs around four hundred dollars, because they are not using the funeral home, and we are not putting in our professional service time. But a traditional funeral, with a wake, embalming, selection of a casket, cemetery cost, newspaper notices, church expenses — usually the total cost of that can be anywhere between two thousand and twenty-five hundred dollars. In a city like Cambridge, cremation costs are about a hundred and fifty dollars, but if you have to purchase a grave and bury someone, it costs between six hundred and eleven hundred dollars, plus also the eventual cost of purchasing a stone."

People spend thousands of dollars a year on funeral preparations, including things like caskets, gravestones, and limousine rentals. Many confused feelings result from the death of a loved one, and this may cause people to spend more money than they should. Dozens of important decisions must be made regarding funerals and burials, and they all must be carefully considered. Funerals are one of the largest single expenses people ever have to face.

GRAVEYARDS

After we interviewed a funeral director, we went to visit a cemetery mason, who makes some of the gravestones for the cemetery. The mason's office was located across from the gates of the cemetery. People come here to decide what kind of stone they want, either for themselves or for a relative who has died. The mason has 300 sample gravestones in the backyard, all of different shapes, sizes, colors, and designs. The actual stones are cut elsewhere, but the mason orders the stones once people have decided what information they want on them.

The first thing a stonecutter does is make a full-size sketch of what will be on the stone with a stencil. Then, from the sketch, a rubber mold is made and put on a granite headstone. A sandblaster, which projects a stream of sand at high speed, is used to cut the design into the granite. Most headstones take three to four weeks to be finished. Prices vary from $300 to $400 for flat markers, to up to $3,000 for large stones for family graves. The cost depends on whether or not the stone is polished, if there is any design to be handcarved on it, and on the number of words used. Most gravestones list the deceased person's name and birth and death dates, and some include something memorable about the person's life, a special poem he or she liked, or any special talents he or she had. We were told that every gravestone has to have a concrete foundation, which costs $300 to $600 and goes four to six feet below the ground at the head of the grave. Every grave also has to have a concrete lining. Graves are so close to each other that there are only two to three inches between each grave.

FUNERALS

Along with choosing the kind of casket, gravestone, and burial site they want, people have to decide whether or not to have a funeral and what kind it will be. Most funerals last about a half-hour or so, and are held in churches or synagogues. The priest or rabbi stands up in front of the room and speaks about the person who has died. The family and friends come to listen and see other people who share their feelings of loss and sadness about the dead person. It is traditional to wear black, the color of mourning.

A funeral can be a very important part of helping a child deal with death. When a special person or pet dies, a child might want a funeral to take place soon, to help focus his or her feelings. Some children find a funeral comforting because it gives them an opportunity to feel sad and admit the feelings of loss. However, other children feel that funerals make everything uncomfortable and too dramatic.

Jamey wrote about her grandfather's funeral, which took place a few months ago: "The funeral of my grandfather was at ten o'clock on a Wednesday morning in a small town in southern Louisiana. My grandma, mother, aunts, uncles, all my cousins, and I got ready at about nine. I wore a brown, flower-print dress. Then we went to church.

"There were a lot of flowers sent by people from throughout the town. I sat in the first row with all my relatives. First a preacher came up and spoke a little about Pappy, and what he was like and how he helped everybody. There were a lot of people at the funeral. The church was pretty full. Charlotte Richardson, a woman who lives in the town my grandmother lived in, sang all the hymns. My dad played the piano for all the songs. Then another priest talked some about my grandfather. Pappy and I were very close so I cried a little, but I wasn't embarrassed because everyone else was crying, too. Then Charlotte Richardson sang again. After that, the church part of the funeral ended.

"We all passed by the casket on the way out and saw my grandfather from the chest up. I felt weird seeing him there. Then my grandmother got in the limousine, and all my relatives and I followed her all the way to Pollock, Texas, where Pappy wanted to be buried. They put the casket into a big metal box called a vault. They lowered it into the ground right next to Pappy's parents. This was a very sad day, but I think it was a good experience for me. This was my first funeral and the first time a person close to me had died. It was a good experience because I learned about how people feel when a loved one dies, and I learned this is a comforting and supportive environment."

Nat wrote about his great-grandmother's funeral: "The funeral took place at Emmanuel Temple Church and one of the many ministers there was my great-uncle. He gave the remarks and messages, and then many other ministers spoke about my great-grandmother. A lady sang 'Amazing Grace' and 'In Times Like These.' She sang beautifully and many people cried. I was very sad and I cried also. The church was packed with friends and relatives and other people who loved my great-grandmother.

"After the ceremony, everyone drove to the cemetery. My great-uncle then spoke again and the casket was lowered into the grave. I noticed that everyone was sad and that many people cried during the funeral. My uncle tried to cheer my cousins up.

"I thought that the funeral was important to me because it showed me how many people loved Grannie. It also brought the family together. I think that Grannie's death was a relief for her because she had been very sick.

"I think funerals can be helpful to kids because they can make you realize that you should love your relatives, so that when they die, they will leave many people who loved them."

We asked Macy to tell us about her grandfather's funeral. She told us that it was a Catholic funeral, and that Catholic churches usually have statues of saints and candles on the altar and other places in the church. The windows of the church were stained glass and there was a big pipe organ in the back of the room. "One thing I didn't like," Macy said, "was when they wheeled the casket in and the priest said,

'Hail the entry of this man!' " Macy thought this sounded too formal.

The priest next sprinkled incense all over the casket. Around this time, Macy noticed that many people were crying, and she said that it made her nervous. The priest spoke about Macy's grand-father going to heaven and said that everyone who is good is sent to heaven after he or she dies, as a reward by God.

Macy told us: "The priest then went on about how we shall all, when the time comes, cross the River of Glory and make it to the second life." This means that we can all expect to die one day. This was the end of the church part of the funeral.

Next, the body was taken out to the cemetery, where there was a canopy over the open grave. Everybody threw flower arrangements onto the ground around the grave. The priest then gave everybody a carnation. Next, the casket was put into the grave, and people threw their carnations on top of the casket.

The priest read from his Bible, and then he took a handful of holy sand and said, "From ashes to ashes, dust to dust," and dropped it onto the casket. This means that people are born out of the earth and return to it when they die.

Macy did not find the funeral very helpful. She found it boring. When she tried to pay attention to what the priest was saying, it didn't seem to make any sense to her. But because Macy was the only child present at the funeral, she did feel important and grown-up. She liked getting the chance to drive around in a black limousine but, in general, thought the funeral was not helpful for her.

Some people don't go to a friend's or relative's funeral, because they think it will be depressing, or they don't want to face death in this way. But funerals are a way for all the friends and relatives of the dead person to get together and share the sadness and release the anger they may feel. A person can find comfort and strength at a funeral.

CREMATION

An alternative to burial is cremation. In the cremation process, a body is placed in its pine coffin inside an incinerator, which is a large brick chamber with gas jets along each side. The doors are shut and the temperature is set to 2,000°F. It takes an hour and forty-five minutes to reduce a body to ashes and small bone fragments. These are placed in an urn or box and can be buried in a grave. People who go to cremation services stay in the chapel and do not see any of the things we have just described. Some people prefer this method over burial, because there is no body left in the ground to decompose and take up space. In some countries, such as Japan and England, most people are cremated when they die. In our country, only about ten percent of the dead are cremated — however, more and more people are choosing to be cremated now than ever before. This is becoming a real problem for undertakers, because it cuts down on their business. With cremation, there is no need for embalming, a casket, or a gravestone. The average cost for cremation is about $300, a bargain compared to the average cost of a funeral and burial.

ORGAN DONATION

Some people believe that, instead of being buried or cremated when they die, it would be more helpful to people who are living if they donated certain parts of their bodies to research and science.

There are many ways of doing this. Some people prefer to donate only certain parts of their bodies, since there are many special banks and organizations that store and offer organs for transplant and medical research. Many parts of the body may be donated. For instance, a person may donate his or her eyes to an eyebank, or skin to a burn institute, where it is used for grafting onto burned patients. Brains may be donated to various tissue resource centers. While a person is still living, he or she can contact a specific organ bank, and receive a contract or information concerning the donation of the organ(s). Later, when a person has decided definitely to donate an organ, he or she may file a witnessed claim, making the donation official. Donations are taken only after death, and the donor may change his or her mind at any time.

Another way to donate a certain organ is to indicate interest on your driver's license. A letter specifying the organ that will be taken (*k* for kidney, *b* for brain, *u* for unlimited) is written on the license. Then, if the donor is killed in an accident, an organ bank may remove the organ specified on the license. The letter can be removed from the license if the donor changes his or her mind.

Still others donate their entire bodies to schools, where they are dissected and tested by students for research.

WILLS

A will is something a person writes or records that declares what should be done with his or her possessions after death. Most wills are formal, legal documents, written with the advice of a lawyer.

Before parents make out a will, it might be helpful to tell the kids they are doing it and to explain what a will is. They should be sure to say that this doesn't mean that they are going to die soon. Parents need not necessarily tell the kids where the will is or what's in it, though they might choose to do so.

One aspect of the will that kids should have input on is who they'll live with if their parents die. The parents should discuss possibilities with the kids, since they would be affected by the new living situation. Parents should also be sure to discuss this with the potential new guardians of the child. Of course, the amount of input the child has will depend on his or her level of maturity.

All parents should feel obligated to make a will, because their deaths will affect a lot of people. Without a will, fights might start among the surviving family members. Property could get into the wrong hands. Parents should also be sure to keep their wills up-to-date, especially if they acquire more possessions, or if there are more children added to the family.

We talked with Barbara Hayes Buell, our school's attorney, about what happens when someone dies without a will. She told us: "If they have more than two thousand dollars in possessions it has to be *probated* — which means the court has to be told who it is going to. If they haven't left a will, the court follows certain rules to determine who gets the possessions. If they have only a spouse, all their things — property, house, pets — go to the spouse, but if they have a spouse and children, the spouse gets half and the children divide the other half. If the dead person is not married, but they have a living mother and/or father, then the parents get all their possessions. If they have no parents, but they have brothers and sisters, then they get the person's possessions. There are a whole lot of rules of inheritance, and each state's rules are slightly different."

We asked Barbara whether a divorced parent can leave the children in the care of a guardian, rather than the other parent. She said, "If someone wants their kids to be taken care of by a certain person, they can only suggest it in their will. If there is another parent who has the right to raise the kids, then the parent who dies can't give them to someone else. For instance, if a parent who is divorced dies, they might not want the other parent to raise the children, but the other parent has that right."

We also asked her about what happens if the family doesn't agree with what's contained in the will. Barbara told us: "They mostly have to go along with it, unless it is shown that the person was crazy or was forced to write what they wrote. Then the will would be thrown out, and, if there was another will which the person had written, it would become the valid will. Also, if someone gets something in a will that they don't want, they can either take it and sell it or they can disclaim their inheritance and, if they do, it will go to another person."

Barbara went on to say that, in order to write a

legal will, you have to be eighteen years old. She told us that a child's possessions go to the parents and siblings. "If there are living parents, the parents get everything that the child had," Barbara said. "If the possessions aren't worth at least two thousand dollars, the estate doesn't have to go through formal probate. Some kids have stocks and bonds that grandparents have given them, worth more than two thousand dollars. The court requires the parents to tell the stock people who the new owner of the stock is."

Some kids feel that they should be able to leave some sort of will. Children who have inherited or made a lot of money might want to leave it to someone in particular, or donate it to charity. Kids could simply have a conversation with their parents and tell them what they want to happen to their possessions after they die, instead of writing a will. It might be a good experience for kids to have, because they would have to face up to the fact that death is a part of life. Kids' wills could be different from adults', because they might divide things based on friendship rather than on obligation. In a way, kids' wills might be more sincere.

Although it is helpful to talk and learn about death in general — what it is and what happens when we die — in order to fully understand death, kids should think about it in terms of themselves and the people around them. Caleb's pediatrician, Dr. Sherry, had this to say: "One thing you ought to think about is separation. Because children hate to be separated from their parents and death is the final separation. . . ." This separation from our loved ones is what makes death very scary to us.

❧ 4 ❧

When Your Pet Dies

OFTEN a child's first experience with the death of a loved one is when a pet dies. Sometimes, when children are very young, they are not fully aware of what is going on.

Caleb: "I used to have a baby garter snake who escaped through the grill on top of his cage. The day after his escape, I stepped on him as I was getting out of bed. The next day, he died. His death didn't mean too much to me then because I hadn't had him long, and that type of snake is hard to feed, anyway. I think it would have been better if it had died from hunger, or on its own in the wild, rather than under a foot."

Older children might be more aware of what is happening when a pet dies and find it a very painful and upsetting experience.

Tanya: "I had a pet teddy-bear hamster for over three years, and so I was very close to him. After a period of time, my teddy-bear hamster just seemed to be slowing down to the point where he would hardly move at all. One day, my friend Sarah and I went to a dance class and, when we returned home, I went to check on my hamster, since he was so sick. He wasn't moving at all, and seemed to be dead. I kept trying and trying to make him move, even though he was dead. The reason I did that, I think, is because I was so close to my hamster, I just couldn't believe that he was dead. I think that it might have been easier for me if he had just died, without me watching him die over a period of time."

Why do animals die? This may be one of the first questions that children ask when they lose a pet.

Pets usually do not live as long as most humans. A healthy, well-cared-for dog, for example, may live about thirteen years. A cat may also live this long. The number of years that a pet may live is called its *lifespan,* and has a lot to do with the kind of animal that it is. A goldfish, for instance, has a lifespan of about a year. See the accompanying table for the lifespans of various animals.

Pets sometimes do not live as long as their lifespan indicates they should, because they may die from accidents or get sick. A car may run over an animal, or an animal may eat rat poison or a poi-

LIFESPANS OF VARIOUS ANIMALS, IN YEARS

Box Turtles	123 years
Humans (U.S.A.)	72$\frac{1}{2}$
Horses	20–30
Cats	13–17
Dogs	12–13
Hermit Crabs	10
Garter Snakes	6
Guinea Pigs	5–6
Gerbils	3–4
Rats	1–2
Mice	1–2
Hamsters	1$\frac{1}{2}$

Source: World Book Encyclopedia, 1970 and 1979.

sonous plant. There is just no telling how your pet is going to die or how long your pet will live. But if you spend all of your time worrying about when your pet is going to die, you won't be able to enjoy it while it is alive.

JOY AND KATE'S EXPERIENCES WITH THE DEATH OF THEIR PETS

The earliest experience with death that Joy remembers was when she was about eight years old. Two of her dogs died. One of them was Charlie, a female Bedlington terrier. The other one was Blue, Charlie's mother.

One day, when Joy was arriving home from school,

her aunt told her to stay out of the house. Joy saw her mother run out the front door with Blue in her arms, and she began to worry. Blue was shaking and making weird noises. Joy's mother got in their car and drove off, heading for the vet. Blue died in Joy's mother's arms on the way. It was too late to save her.

When her mother came home she was crying. Joy didn't know what was going on, but her mother told her that Blue was dead. Joy and her family went outdoors and walked around the Bunker Hill Monument together to try to let their feelings and sadness out.

Charlie died three years after Blue died. She died a slow death. When Charlie started vomiting and drinking out of the fishbowl, Joy knew that she was sick. Joy's family took her to the vet, and the veterinarian showed them what her gums and the whites of her eyes looked like. Her gums were bright yellow, and so were her eyeballs. Joy decided to leave her there so the vet could look at her and see if she would get better. A day later when Joy's mother called the vet to see if Charlie was okay, the vet told Joy's mother that Charlie had died in her sleep. Joy really loved Charlie and started to cry very hard. It took Joy a long time to get over Charlie's death.

Kate's grandmother had a dog named Cocoa, who died when Kate was about five years old. Cocoa had heart trouble and had to be given an injection which caused him to die quickly and peacefully. Kate's mother told her Cocoa had died, and Kate immediately ran to her grandmother. She remembers being very sad and crying, but that is all.

When Kate was ten, Ginger, her guinea pig, died. Ginger had been lying in her cage when Kate left for school and she thought Ginger was just sleeping. But after school, at four o'clock, Ginger was still lying in the same place. Kate opened the cage and Ginger still didn't move, so Kate picked the animal up. When she still didn't move, and Kate saw that Ginger's feet were all scrunched up, Kate screamed and dropped her. Kate ran downstairs and began to cry. Half an hour later or so, Kate put Ginger in a shoebox, tied it with a ribbon, and buried Ginger under a tree in her yard.

How Kids Should Be Told

From Kate and Joy's stories, it is clear that the way in which we find out that a pet has died is an important factor in our reaction to the death. If you see a pet die suddenly, or witness the drawn-out death of the animal, it is much different than when the news is presented to you by someone else, like a parent or a veterinarian. There are many ways parents can tell their kids that a pet has died. Some ways are helpful, and others are not.

Deirdre Leopold (Kate's mother) recently told

Kate's sister Holly — who is eight years old — that her pet hamster died. At the time, Holly was visiting at her grandparents' house. Deirdre explained over the telephone how Molly, the hamster, died. She said that Molly had suffocated under a house in her cage. Holly's first reaction was to feel sad, and she cried immediately. Her next reaction was that she wanted to tell her sister Kate right away.

Deirdre put Molly's body in a shoebox and put it outside so that the cats couldn't get to it. Deirdre wanted to give Holly the time to decide what to do with the body. Deirdre told us: "It was sad for me to clean out Molly's cage and put it downstairs. We had gotten her some hamster treats and she never had a chance to eat them." Deirdre also said that she would have preferred to have Molly die from natural causes.

Holly's mother treated Molly's death with sensitivity. A less effective way for parents to inform their child would be to say something like, "Hey, your dog died yesterday and I'll get you a new one next week," in a happy tone. The kid might not want a dog to replace the old one right away. Also, it is best to prepare the child for hearing about the death, rather than just announce it suddenly.

Macy thinks that parents should explain the situation to their kids, if their pet becomes sick. The parents should be honest and tell exactly what condition the pet is in, and not lie. Jamey says that there are some times when maybe a parent should tell a white lie. If the pet was hit by a car, for example, or experienced another kind of violent death, it might come as a great shock to the kid, and the parents might choose to cover up how it happened. Jamey thinks that once the kid gets used to being without the pet, the parents could then tell the kid the whole truth, and also explain why they didn't tell him or her earlier.

Another way in which a parent might tell the child about the pet's death would be to use a soothing tone of voice, so the kid won't get terribly upset. Peter Richards, a teacher we know, suggested that the parent hold the kid's hand or put an arm around the child, while telling him or her what happened, so the child feels more comfortable.

It is also important to find the right place to tell the child about the death of a pet. A place like the living room would be nice, because it is familiar and it would feel better there. A child's bedroom is also a good place. If a child receives bad news in a public place (like in an elevator or subway), he or she may not feel comfortable showing his or her true feelings.

When a pet dies at an animal hospital, there are also good ways for the veterinarian to inform the family. We interviewed Dr. Yashar Bahceli, a vet who works near our school. He described how he tells people this kind of news. Dr. Bahceli approaches the subject very slowly and carefully, explaining first what was wrong with the animal. After he goes over this in detail, he then tells the owners that the pet is dead. Dr. Bahceli says this is hard for him to do. All of us should keep in mind that this is difficult information to have to report, and that the vet has done his or her best in breaking it to you.

KIDS' FEELINGS ABOUT A PET DYING

There are many different emotions you may feel when your pet dies. Anger is one of them. You may be mad that your pet is not with you anymore and never will be again. You may be angry at whoever caused the pet to die. Kids also often feel sad when a pet dies. Even if you know your pet will die soon, it can still be a shock to realize that you will never cuddle or talk to that pet again. Sometimes you never even have the chance to say good-bye.

Some kids may even want to deny the truth, at first. Mindy Sobota's dog, Mao-Mao, had cancer, and the vets first thought they had gotten all the cancer out through an operation. Later they found more. Mao-Mao was in pain, and Mindy felt really sorry for him. Still, her first reaction when she heard Mao-Mao had died was, "I don't believe he's dead." If Mao-Mao had not been in pain, Mindy would rather have had him be with her when he died.

Guilt is another common feeling kids have. A class of five-, six-, and seven-year-olds in our school immediately wanted to know from their teacher, Fern Fisher, if their class pet, a gerbil, had died because of something they had done. This is usually not the case, but it is common for kids to feel guilty for not caring for the pet properly, or for not being sweet to the pet all the time.

If your pet has just died, you might even feel jealous of your friends who have pets. This situation is made even worse if a friend talks about his or her living pets. You might feel very jealous and angry, even though you really like the person. If this happens, your friend may be totally unaware of what you're feeling, so you might want to remind him or her that your pet has recently died. If your friend is a good one, he or she will know when to stop talking.

GERBIE'S DEATH

Gerbie was a gerbil living in Fern Fisher's classroom. Gerbie was very old, and as we were writing this book, he became quite sluggish and weak. The class wondered if he would ever get well, but he slowly became weaker and weaker, and soon he died.

Fern handled the whole situation very well with the class. Kate visited Fern's class for the meeting in which Fern first told the kids that Gerbie was dying. The class was aware already that Gerbie was sick. Fern slowly told them that Gerbie was very old and that he would die. Fern let her class ask questions, and then the class wrote poems about the gerbil.

Here is a poem written by Judy Grant, one of the children in Fern's class:

Bye, Gerby
I hope I see you in heaven.
I love you just about more than anything.
I never knew a gerbil more talented.
I wish you could stay.
If there was anything I could do I would do it.
I hope you have had a nice long life.
You are more beautiful than a flock of birds.

After Gerbie died, Fern's class had another meeting. Fern asked if some of them wanted to see Gerbie one last time. Many children did. She also asked them to think of some items they might want to bury with Gerbie. Some of the things they thought of were: food, money, and his little house, which a child had given him the day before.

WILLY DOG'S DEATH

Willy was a dog that was with our school for twelve years. He was a big black dog, with big paws and furry ears. He didn't belong to anyone at Fayer-weather, but every day Willy would walk to school and stay for the day. He would sit out on the porch in the sun or walk around the classrooms. He was considered a member of our school's community and was even allowed to graduate from the school after he attended classes for nine years.

During lunchtime, Willy played with kids, catching rocks, playing chase, or enjoying some other game. Some kids gave him sandwiches or other bits of their lunches. A few kids even went out to Leo's, a market near the school, and bought Willy some ham or liver. Sometimes Leo would save a particularly juicy bone for Willy, and Willy would carry it back to the schoolyard.

On February 7, 1982, while we were writing this book, Willy was hit by a car and his leg was broken in three places.

Willy had two operations on his leg. On February 18, he died in his sleep. As far as the doctors knew, it was a painless death, but we were all very, very sad.

We had a big school meeting to share our feelings about Willy's death. Debby, a girl in our class, wrote a song about Willy. Several kids who heard the song cried. Debby told us, "Writing the song about Willy helped me to cope with my feelings about his death." Gillian, another girl in our school, wrote a poem about Willy.

Some people in our class wrote papers about Willy that helped us remember the good times with him:

Nathan: "When I heard that Willy had died, I felt very sad. It is very hard for me to have known Willy so long and then have someone tell me that he is dead. I remember the first time that I ever saw Willy, I was about four years old and I was visiting the school. It was during a Friday when everyone was at school meeting. I was sitting with my brother, and Willy walked into the room and sat down right next to me. Ever since then, I really liked Willy. I wish that he had never gotten into the car accident, so he wouldn't have had to get surgery and die. But I think that I did not feel as bad as I would have if the teachers had told us differently. I think we were told in the best possible way."

Elizabeth: "Willy was great. I'll never forget him. Whenever I pass the meat counter at Leo's I'll think of him being so happy that he jumped all over me. I'll think of coming to school and not seeing him there on the sidewalk, panting. I will always remember the tricks I taught him and the way everybody griped to me about feeding him ham. I wish I could have said good-bye to him. Everyone says that he died in his sleep, peacefully, but that still means that I'll never see him again.

"When Eric told everybody about Willy dying, my stomach felt really tight. I started crying and feeling sad and happy at the same time, but more sad, of course. I was happy because he died naturally without any shots, but sad for me and all the other kids who would miss him. Somebody said something funny at the meeting and I had to laugh. I really felt unloyal doing that in the middle of feeling sorry for myself.

"Willy wasn't a 'cute' dog, or a 'pretty' dog. He was a very special Willy dog."

WILLY DOG

A song by Debby Alexander

If you hear a death, so far away
It's so hard to recognize;
For you can't see it near,
'Cause death's so far away, so far away from home.

Willy dog just left us sitting here
    watching the sky.
A little anger always falls in with a lot of sadness.
A long life is worth the wait, just don't die slowly,
    don't die slowly.

Willy dog is just so far away
I wonder where he'll settle now, so far away.
And sadness fills our grief of him,
Doesn't last as long as we think of him.

Remember Willy dog,
Remember him.

Remember Willy dog,
Remember him.
And so far away,
But so close . . .
Can't believe we'll never see him again.

ANIMALS "PUT TO SLEEP"

Sometimes, when a pet gets very old or very sick, you may have to make a decision to "put the animal to sleep." This means that the vet gives the animal a shot that kills it. This is a very serious and sad thing to do, and something families often think about for quite a while. You have to decide if you want the pet to live in a weakened, sick condition, or if you want to put an end to its suffering. It is called "putting an animal to sleep" because some people think of death as an endless sleep. But the pet does not go to sleep, it dies, and so the phrase "putting an animal to sleep" may give a false impression.

It's usually very painful to know that your pet was killed because it was very, very sick. But it is also a relief to know that the animal will no longer suffer. Dorothy, a girl in our class, had to make a choice about whether or not to help her pet die quickly and painlessly.

When Dorothy was nine years old, she had a cat named Socrates. Socrates was a stray cat, and when

Dorothy first saw him she knew she wanted to adopt him. Socrates was small and acted like a kitten. Dorothy assumed he was young, but the cat actually was old and had kidney troubles. Shortly after she adopted the cat, Dorothy took him to the vet, because he began to get really sick. He was so sick, in fact, that the vet had to inject food into him, because he could not digest regular cat food. Dorothy and her family were faced with a difficult choice: whether to keep Socrates living in this condition or to help him die. They were told Socrates would not get well. Dorothy decided that seeing the cat in pain was horrible. And Socrates couldn't enjoy life in the state he was in. Dorothy thought it best to take him to the vet to be given a death-inducing injection, because nothing more could help.

MOURNING AND BURIAL

After a pet has died, often children may want to bury the pet in a backyard or a park with a quiet funeral. (Some towns, however, may have laws restricting this kind of burial.)

You can gather together all the people who were close to the pet — your family, friends, classmates. People might want to prepare poems, stories, or songs about the pet before the funeral.

Before your pet has been put in a shoebox or carton, we suggest you first wrap the body in something, such as a paper towel, cloth, or plastic bag. Then dig a deep hole and place the box in it. Then, as you fill in the hole, perhaps people can say a prayer, read poems or stories, sing a song, or have a silent moment in which to remember your pet.

Burial is only one way to say good-bye to a pet. Cremation is another alternative. The body can be burned, and the ashes can be kept in a jar or sprinkled over one of your pet's favorite places. If you are considering cremation, we suggest you look under "Pet Cemeteries" in the Yellow Pages.

Mounting is another option. The body of the animal can be stuffed and displayed in an airtight case. This was done with Trigger, Roy Rogers's horse. The disadvantage to mounting is that it can be more expensive than both burial and cremation. For instance, mounting a parakeet costs approximately $85. A house cat costs between $350 and $500, and $900 and up is the price for a dog. The advantage is that a mounted pet should last indefinitely. If you'd like to look into this further, we again suggest the Yellow Pages as a place to start.

There is no best way to mourn your pet. Give yourself time to remember your pet — the good times and the bad. Talk about the pet with friends and family. You might even make a memorial statue. Mourning your pet has to be done in your own way, to suit your own needs.

PET HEAVEN

Some people think pet heaven is the place where pets go when they die.

Helene Stern, Joy's aunt, believes in pet heaven. She told us that she believes a "journeyman" meets the animal after it dies and takes it to the next level of life. In order to get there, the animal has to pay some money, so an animal should be buried with two coins in its mouth to pay for the ticket to the next level. Helene told us that this idea comes from ancient Greece.

We've asked many kids to tell us what they think of pet heaven. One five-year-old girl in our school said that she doesn't believe in pet heaven. She thinks the body of the animal stays in the ground and slowly becomes part of the soil. Darya, a seven-year-old, thinks the animal's body stays in the ground and the spirit goes to heaven. Dorothy, a thirteen-year-old, says that pet heaven is whatever anybody imagines it to be.

❧ 5 ❧

The Death of Older Relatives and Parents

THE DEATH OF OLDER RELATIVES

AFTER the death of a pet, the death of a grand-parent or great-grandparent is probably the most common experience with death that kids have.

When grandparents or other older relatives die, children often do not react as strongly as their parents. This may be because the kids don't know the deceased as well as their parents do. Also, it's more expected for grandparents to die, because they're older. Sometimes kids may feel guilty about their lack of feeling.

Once Macy's father made her a dollhouse, and her grandfather promised her "all the furniture she'd ever want." He died after the dollhouse was finished, and Macy, who was eight, felt bad because she wasn't going to get all the doll furniture. She ended up feeling guilty because the only reason she felt upset about the death was the loss of the furniture.

When Seth's grandfather died, Seth was at a friend's house. His mother called and Seth was very surprised to hear about the death. Then he felt guilty because he wasn't sadder.

Kama told us this story about her great-grandmother's death, and about how she felt she reacted in a strange way:

"My great-grandmother died three years ago in June. My great-grandmother had been very ill for a pretty long time. I didn't get to see her very much before she died, because she was in the hospital.

"One night I was sitting down on my grandmother's bed, watching television. My grandmother sat down beside me and said, 'Your great-grandmother is probably going to die tonight.' I just sat there and looked at her. I wanted to cry but I couldn't. I don't know why, but I just couldn't cry. I went to bed very upset that night.

"In the morning, I woke up and went into my grandmother's room and I asked her if my great-grandmother died, and she said, 'No, not yet, luckily.'

"Three days passed, and as each day went by I knew it was closer for my great-grandmother to die. One day I went to my aunt's house, and when I walked in, all my aunts and other relatives were there, and my grandmother and grandfather were there, too. Everyone was just sitting there and some people were crying. I knew at that time that she had died. All I could think of was telling my friends.

"On the day of the funeral, I got all dressed up and went. When I got there, that's when I started to cry. Just seeing her lying there in the coffin, I felt really upset."

If a grandparent has been very sick for a long period of time, a child might feel relieved when the grandparent dies. Caleb told us this story about visiting his grandfather before he died:

"When my grandfather died, it was upsetting to me, but I think it was more upsetting to my father. When he died he was sixty-five or sixty-six years old and had been in the hospital, on and off, for a long time. I don't know how it was discovered, but about six months before his death, he was found to have brain cancer. He was hospitalized and many tests were done and he started receiving medicine. Later, he started getting chemotherapy, and I think, soon after, I went down to New York and visited him in the hospital. He was very thin and didn't have much color, and he had lost his hair from the tests and radiation treatment. It felt sad and depressing to see him like that. Later, he was allowed to go home and a nurse visited him daily and he still went into the hospital for chemotherapy.

"We came and visited him after he had moved to my uncle's house. Whenever we went, I always hated it because he would fall asleep while talking, which he didn't do much of, and I would be called into his room and try to have a conversation with him, which never worked. My father would have to feed him and push him around in a wheelchair, until finally he couldn't move from his bed. Soon he was taken to the hospital where he died. Whenever we went to see him, it was always sad and usually depressing. I was upset when he died, but not really all that sad because I was never really extra-close to him."

We wondered about how old people feel, knowing that they might die at any time. As part of our research, we visited Norma Farber, a woman in her seventies, who lived near our school in a modern building by the Charles River. When we visited her, she told us about her four children and seven grandchildren, and she said that her husband had died several years ago.

We thought Mrs. Farber was a very interesting person. When she was young she wanted to be an opera singer, but she ended up being a very successful writer instead. She wrote nineteen children's books and nine adult books, including poetry. She wrote a book called *How Does It Feel to Be Old?*, which we have all read and enjoyed.

We asked Mrs. Farber if she was afraid of dying. She told us, "I am not afraid of dying because I feel that I have led a rich life and have completed everything that I have wanted to do. I live each day as it comes, and I fill it up doing different things. I know that each day may be my last day, or it may be my second-to-last day, but I don't live my life worrying about it."

After our interview, we decided that Mrs. Farber was very lucky to be in her position. She made it clear that if she had not completed everything that she had wanted to, she would have felt a lot worse thinking about dying.

Even if a child is not close to an older relative, or even if the person's death is expected, the news may still come as a shock, and whoever has to break the news should keep this in mind.

Macy remembers when her mother's cousin's wife died, and her father told her about it in the family car:

"My father had just picked me up from a friend's house because we had gone skiing, and I was really excited about seeing him again. After a while we were both quiet and finally he told me that she died. It was a shock to me, because he just came out and said it and, for a minute, I thought I had heard him wrong. I felt like I should say something, but I just said, 'Oh no!' "

Lots of kids are put in a situation similar to Macy's, in which they feel as if they should say something, but are not quite sure what it should be. This can sometimes make a child say something that isn't at all appropriate at the time. The child shouldn't feel obligated to say anything if he or she doesn't want to.

When Elizabeth's great-grandmother died, her grandmother took her to a bookshop and bought her a book called *Why Did God Let Grandpa Die?*, and then she told Elizabeth that her great-grandmother had died. Elizabeth didn't say anything, she just started to cry.

The way Elizabeth's grandmother told her was very good, and later on Elizabeth said that the book her grandmother had purchased helped her cope with some of her feelings of pain at the time.

Parents and other relatives should try to help kids after a death, but kids should also remember to comfort their parents. Together both parents and children can try to make the best of a bad situation.

The Death of Parents

Probably every child worries, at some time or another, that something bad will happen to his or her mother and father that will cause them to die. As much as all of us fear this happening, the fact is that most children do *not* experience the death of a parent. Most parents live to see their children grow into adulthood, and many live long enough to become grandparents.

If your father or mother *should* die when you are still a child, however, it may be very traumatic. When a parent dies, it is often difficult to believe, and you may not react for a long time, because you are in such great shock. It is a shock you may never forget or thoroughly get over.

One girl in our class, Debby, who is fourteen years old, experienced the death of her father when she was nine. Her father had undergone five major operations and was taking medicine to prevent blood clots, when he suddenly had a hemorrhage, which is internal bleeding, of the brain, and a seizure, which is an abnormal electrical impulse in the brain. He was forty-one years old when he died.

Macy interviewed Debby about the death of her father, which is still difficult for her to talk about.

Debby told Macy that when she first heard that her father was dead she was shocked and didn't believe it. This was very difficult news for Debby to hear because she was close to her father, and even today, Debby isn't sure if she is over the loss.

After the death, Debby felt very bad and very sorry for herself. She told us that she thinks this is a common reaction. Her brother, who is two years older than Debby, also felt bad, and their mother was very sad and cried a lot. While Debby doesn't remember feeling angry or aggressive toward other people, she does remember feeling a whole lot of pity for herself.

Debby liked the funeral, because the minister was very nice, and because she allowed herself to cry through the ceremony and didn't hold in her feelings. After the death, Debby found that some parts of the family house reminded her of her father and made her sad and depressed, such as her father's bed and his den in their basement. Debby told us: "I never want to move the things in his den around or change them from the way he had them."

One of the reasons it's hard for Debby to talk about her father's death with other people is that she doesn't want everyone to feel sorry for her. Sometimes Debby feels jealous that other kids have a father to do things with.

If Debby could change the way her father died, she'd change it so that she would have been able to say good-bye to him.

The circumstances surrounding the parent's death may also affect how the child reacts. We interviewed one young woman whose mother died in a car accident. She was hit by a car on a rainy night, when she was crossing the street after shopping. The woman we interviewed had been five years old at the time. She told us: "When I was little I felt angry, because I felt the man who killed my mother should be in jail. Now I feel that the man must have nightmares about what happened, and about the poor children whose mother he killed."

Macy thinks suicide is the most emotionally upsetting of deaths. She could never picture anyone unhappy enough to kill him- or herself. She also thinks that a child may worry about inheriting feelings of depression and violence and self-destructiveness from his or her parents.

Annie Fisher, a teacher at Full-Circle School in Somerville, who is now in her thirties, talked about this when she discussed her parents' suicides, one of which (her father's) took place when Annie was a child. She told us: "I don't know what was going on in my father's life at the time, and after his suicide, my brother and I went away for a while. The reason for that was for my mother to get used to his death. It seemed like I was away from her for years. When I was living with her again, I remember asking her one day, 'When's Daddy coming home?,' and she started to cry, so I was afraid to ask her questions. It was only after my mother's funeral that I found out my father shot himself. I think my mother killed herself because she was living a pretty unhappy life. She died of carbon monoxide poisoning in the garage. There have been times when I've often wondered if I would inherit the feelings of depression and self-destruction. It used to scare me, but not anymore. I don't feel at all that ending my life is an option."

A parent dying when a child is a teenager can also be very difficult. A teenager has known his or her parent for a longer time than a younger child, and has a more realistic understanding of death.

Another problem is that, as they get older, kids begin to look at their parents differently from when they were young. Parents are no longer seen as perfect, but as real people who make judgments, decisions, and mistakes.

Linda Brown's father, Caleb's grandfather, died of a heart attack when she was fourteen years old. Linda told us: "I felt very badly, because the night my father died, I went to show him my first pair of high-heel shoes that I was going to wear to a party, and he made a judgment that I thought was not fair. I told him I thought he was a bitch. And when I called my father a bitch, I ran out of the room and went to bed. The next day I went to school, and when I came home my brother was there crying, and I found out that, in fact, my father was dead. So I think my first reaction was, 'Oh my god, he's dead because I swore at him.' And I think for a long time I felt very guilty."

She continued, "I had just begun to know my father and, as most adolescents do, I began to see my parents as people, and not the superheroes I had thought them to be when I was younger. So when my father died, it cut off a whole beginning of getting to know him as a person.

"I think if I could have changed the way he died,

I would have changed it so he was older, and he could have known me better, and I could have known him, because I was just beginning to challenge him."

How Kids Are Told About
a Parent's Death

The way kids are told can make a big difference in the way they feel about the death of a parent.

Annie Fisher's father committed suicide when she was three-and-a-half. She was playing on a swing set with her brother in the backyard at the time. She told us: "When he died, I remember my Aunt Mary came out to get us, and brought us into the house. And I remember my brother was sitting next to her on the couch and I was sitting on her lap, and I remember her saying, 'Your daddy's dead.' And I remember I made a game of it. I said, 'What did you say? What did you say?' over and over again, bouncing up and down on her lap. I was laughing, and I think my brother was, too. I was too young and didn't really understand, and I made a joke out of it."

Our class had various ideas of how to tell kids about a parent's death.

Joy felt that the remaining parent should talk to the child in a quiet place. Every detail should be told about how the death happened, unless some of the information is particularly unpleasant. The parent must use judgment and do his or her best in comforting the child.

Elizabeth felt the remaining parent should tell the kid during a routine activity, such as getting picked up from school, eating snacks, or doing their chores. If the death was an accident, she said the parent should say something like: "Your mommy was in a bad accident, and she won't be coming home because she is dead." Elizabeth felt lying shouldn't even be an option, that a child must be told the truth about the parent's death.

Macy felt if the death of a parent was turning out to be a slow process, as with cancer, the other parent should not lie about what was happening. However, if a parent were to die violently, covering up the truth might be kinder to the child. Macy felt if the parent was murdered, for example, the child might have more anger and fear if he or she were told the truth. This all depends on the age of the child, and how the particular child would handle the actual situation. Parents should try to be honest in expressing their sadness, but they should also be aware that if their children see them cry too much, it might worry the children deeply.

We thought it would be good to include the opinions of some of the people we interviewed, about what can be done to help kids who have experienced the death of one or both of their parents.

Fourteen-year-old Debby felt that advice on how

to help depends on the child or children involved, because, as she said, "Some people like pity, others don't."

Annie suggested this: "I would try to find someone you can trust or feel close with, to talk about your feelings of loss, because those feelings can be tremendously confusing when you are a child. It need not be a psychiatrist, but it should be a caring person, such as a teacher, a counselor, a relative, or a friend. A friend can be very helpful."

"I know what advice I'd give in general," Linda Brown said. "You should do all the loving, and all the caring every day that you can. Because it feels so lousy when a person dies, and you say 'Damn it, *I should have*'; so I think you should lead your life with all the should-haves, and not make excuses for things because death is present. It can happen, and it can happen to anyone. And what's good, if you are being left by death, and a person dies, is that you had leveled with them about your feelings, that you've left things honest and open."

SHOULD A CHILD GO TO THE PARENT'S FUNERAL?

A big question for many families is whether or not the child should "pay last respects" to his or her parent at a funeral. A lot of people believe that, if the child doesn't go to the funeral, it means the child doesn't love or care about the parent. That isn't true. Some kids may prefer not to go to the funeral for many reasons.

In any case, if a parent does die, it should be the child's decision whether or not to go to the funeral.

Elizabeth feels children should be able to go if they understand what a funeral is for. Joy feels it could be good for a child to go to the funeral because it might help him or her to face what has happened. But both Elizabeth and Joy feel the child shouldn't be forced to go.

A lot of parents don't think a very young child should go to a funeral. Macy agrees with this idea to some extent. She feels an infant shouldn't go, because he or she wouldn't understand what was happening, and would only get bored and fidgety and distract people. But if the child is old enough to be aware of what has happened, then he or she should have the option of going.

Annie was three and a half years old and didn't go to her father's funeral, because her mother thought she was too young. She did go to her mother's funeral when she was eighteen.

"At my mother's funeral, I was very conscious of trying to take care of different people," she told us, "which was also a way of taking care of me. I think it really bothered me to see so many people upset over a person's death. And I had never seen my brother cry, except when he fell down and scraped his knee."

Linda Brown's father's funeral was much different from Annie's mother's funeral. Linda told us: "The funeral was in my home. I remember feeling numb because this big event was happening at a very painful time. It bothered me because, there was this box, this casket, and I knew my father was in that casket. And it wasn't an open-casket funeral. So there weren't people walking around the casket, staring into it. And I had not gone to the funeral home the night before the funeral to see my father inside the casket.

"I had a very unusual experience. My aunt, my father's sister, was very affected by the death of her brother. She explained to me in minute detail what my father *looked* like as a dead person. That was also very hard for me, because I did want to remember my father as I knew him.

"My brothers and I had the privilege and the option to go to the funeral home if we wanted to. My mother didn't think children should go, but if we wanted to, we could. I had already been filled with stories by my aunt, so I decided I didn't want to go to the funeral home.

"The funeral itself was very beautiful. There were hundreds and hundreds of yellow roses everywhere, and the house was very bright, with sunlight coming in everywhere. And in the Jewish faith, there is also a week where you spend some time sitting on a special bench, it's called 'sitting shivah,' and people come and visit and give their sympathy. And you sit in your living room, or your den, and maybe hundreds of people will come each day. Many people did come, and that helped to loosen up some of my feelings — listening to people talk about my father as a 'wonderful, kind person,' and they were also very kind to me, and helped me with some of the sadness I felt. I didn't go to school those two weeks, and some of my friends came to see me and sat with me."

WHERE DO PARENTS GO WHEN THEY DIE?

Lots of kids have different opinions about where their parent has gone once he or she has died. Some kids believe their parent just goes to sleep, and some believe the parent goes to heaven. A more interesting and creative belief some kids have is that the parent's body is nothing but a mask, and it means nothing when the parent is displayed at a funeral home, because the real soul of the parent is somewhere else.

Debby wrote this interesting poem after her father died:

My dad is gone today
but the memories which will always stay
the goodness, the happiness,
the loud times, the badness,
the peace of mind, the quiet times,
where has it all gone,
in my memories I hope.
He's gone but his memories will always stay.
The feelings about him, and the times we had.
Now sadness and frustration follows.
Memories.
Is death bad or sweet?
White *or pure?*
Should it be anticipated or hated for removing my dad?
Is death a happening *with no fault?*
I love my dad and always will.
He is gone, and I will see him when I go too.
Is death a time of logic and thought?
Will I see my grandma and grandpa and other ones
    I have lost in the past?
Should I fear the place of my dog who's going now,
or feel good for her,
for peace of life is coming?

When a parent dies, a child may want to write a
poem or do a piece of artwork to express his or her
feelings at that time. This is good, inexpensive therapy, and it has helped a lot of kids we know.

When Linda's father died, she had a hard time

getting adjusted to the change of a parent being gone, and for a while she really believed that he would come back. She said, "There were some constant reminders, kind of like a void, when my father would be present. Things like when we ate at six o'clock. Also, before dinner my father would have a glass of sherry and a piece of bologna. And I was so used to that, that after he died, a very long tradition no longer existed. And I think it was hard to sit at the table for a while, because Daddy was no longer there."

SCHOOLMATE REACTIONS

After a parent dies, the child usually takes time off from school. This can be very helpful, because he or she has time to experience all the feelings in private. When the time comes to go back to school, however, the situation is not always pleasant.

Sometimes the teacher will announce to the whole class what has happened, which can be most embarrassing. Teachers should handle this situation by talking with the kid, before making an announcement to the class, to make sure he or she is comfortable with the idea.

Classmates or peers sometimes are afraid to talk to the child, mostly because they think he or she might be depressed, or overly sensitive. Some kids are so disturbed by this that they may want to switch schools, just so they can have friends who will treat them "normally." The feelings of discomfort will go away in time, and switching schools is a dramatic move that is probably not necessary.

The father of a boy in our class was very sick during much of our work on this book. While many of us can imagine how we would feel if we found out that a parent was dying, this boy's family was actually living through this very difficult process. While the man has not died from his illness, through most of the period we worked on the book everyone expected him to die shortly, and the family prepared themselves for this experience.

The Colenbacks are a family of four — a mother named Pat, a father named Don, and two sons: John, who is fourteen and in our class, and Jared, who is eight years old. While we were working on this book, John's family was told by doctors that his father was dying from a brain tumor.

In August 1980, Don Colenback, who is an Episcopal priest, had a seizure while he was driving. Pat thought her husband had had a stroke, and he was taken to a hospital to recover and to have some tests done to find out what was wrong. The doctors performed a brain scan, or X-ray. When Pat was shown the brain scan, she saw a dark shadow across part of the brain. She knew that the shadow meant either that there was a blood clot in Don's brain (which would have caused the stroke), or that he had a brain tumor, which is what it turned out to be.

Don and Pat told us about how difficult it was for them to face the fact that Don had a serious illness. They both tried to deny the full extent of Don's sickness. Pat explained this to us: "The human mind and spirit can sustain only so much shock at one time, so you don't absorb all the information at once. You hear a little bit, sometimes you mishear things, because to hear it correctly is too over-whelming. Day by day, you pick up a little more information. Slowly I started to ask more questions."

We asked Don and Pat about when they first told their children. Pat said that she had been talking to John and Jared a little bit about Don's illness, but not very much until she found out that Don had a brain tumor. She said, "When they did the angio-gram, a very special brain test, and we had the def-inite news that it was a brain tumor, I sat down with my kids and apologized to them because I had prac-tically lived at the hospital." She then asked John and Jared if they had any questions for her.

John said to her, "It's a tumor, isn't it?" Pat told him that he was right. John next said, "That means it's malignant, doesn't it?" Pat said that it was.

Next, Jared asked, "That means Daddy's going to die soon, doesn't it?" Pat told him, "Yes, he won't live for a long time." Then Jared changed the subject, because, Pat thinks, he couldn't deal with anything else at this time.

Later that evening, John asked Pat, "Will we continue living in this house? Will we be able to go to the same school?" Pat told us she thinks John needed to know that, even if the family could not control whether Don lived or died, they could control some things that mattered, including their home and going to school.

Don spent several months very sick in the hospital, followed by radiation treatment to control the size of the tumor. These first months were a very difficult time for the family. Pat told us: "Emotionally, it was so overwhelming that it was like walking through a dream or a nightmare. We sort of tumbled from one day to the next and never thought beyond each day. There was too much that was overwhelming. Daily life, as we knew it ordinarily, just stopped existing. The whole world revolved around things at the hospital and what was happening to Don. It altered our lives very much."

Don said, "It has been almost eighteen months since this sickness entered into our lives. It has really affected the life we have, particularly when I was in the hospital. Pat spent a lot of time with me in the hospital. Fortunately, because we live on the campus of a seminary, there were dozens of students who were helping to run the house — so that Jared and John had plenty of people to look after them."

After several months, it became clear that Don wasn't going to die right away. Pat said, "I realized that no family can go on living like that. We had to begin to live our daily life in a more realistic way. At first it was like handling a glass egg. Everyone was being terribly careful all the time — beyond what you can live with. Now our lives are, in a sense, very much back to what they were, except that maybe we don't let problems ride as long as we would have before. We try to make the best of each day."

Don told us that the experience of thinking that he was dying had a big effect on him. "I did a lot more thinking and feeling about the really important things in my life," he told us. "One of the things I said early on in my illness was that, as hard as it seems to think this way, there are some positive things that happen to you when you're sick like this, along with the negative things. You really concentrate on what's most important to you."

We also asked them about the children's reactions to this experience. Pat said, "The kids generally didn't like to talk a lot about it. School was the one place for John last year where no one knew about it except Eric [our teacher], and so it was a place where he didn't have to think about it."

Don told us: "I chatted with Jared a number of times, like when I put him to bed. I thought it was a good, open conversation. He made it clear when he was finished with the conversation, and he made it very clear he didn't want to discuss my illness more at that time. He started talking about the Celtics game."

Pat pointed out that each of the family members dealt with Don's illness in a different way. "Both Don and I were more comfortable sharing what was happening to us than the boys were," she said. "For John, sharing something like this was very uncomfortable. For him it was a very private matter, and he didn't want to talk about it. Jared was very frightened by it and couldn't talk about it very much."

The death of Pat's mother of lung cancer five years earlier made some things easier for the family to deal with during Don's illness. He told us: "In one way, for John and Jared, their grandmother's death helped to make death a real part of their lives. It's not something that we keep in the closet and never talk about. So even though the threat of death is a terrible thing for them to cope with, if it hadn't been for my mother-in-law's death, it would have been harder."

The experience of Don's illness must have had a great effect on all the people in the Colenback family. To face having a father die is very difficult for a mother and her children, and to have him die slowly must be even more difficult. The Colenbacks have dealt with their situation in a very healthy way.

❧ 6 ❧

The Death of Children

THE death of a peer or sibling is particularly difficult for children to deal with. While it is not common, some children have experienced the death of a classmate, friend, brother, or sister. When this happens, it is very sad and can be very frightening.

It is particularly sad when a child dies, because a child has not had a full chance to enjoy life, and has not been able to see a lot of things that he or she would have if life had been longer. And a child's death is scary for other kids, because it makes them feel vulnerable.

The death of a sibling leaves a great big hole in the family. Usually everyone feels angry and sad. The parents may wonder why God did this to them and feel cheated. The remaining siblings may find that they even miss some of the obnoxious things their brother or sister used to do. Sometimes the family can't help wondering if they are somehow responsible for the child's death. It is natural for many kids to think of all the bad things they did to their brother or sister, and feel sorry or guilty, or to think that, if they had done certain things differently, the sibling wouldn't have died. These are common worries for kids to have after a brother or sister has died, but it is almost always certain that those things they feel guilty about had nothing to do with their brother's or sister's death. All of us fight in one way or another with our siblings, and most of us have managed, so far, to survive. Fighting between brothers and sisters does not normally cause them to die.

If a classmate died, you might feel very bad and find it awkward to look at the classmate's empty desk and think about him or her. If the person was a close friend, you might feel sad and angry, and if the person wasn't close, you might just feel sorry for his or her friends and family. The death might also make you a little scared, because you'd think, "If Jennie died, it could happen to me, too."

In our research for this book we learned that American children die from various causes. Here are the top ten causes of deaths for kids, ages one to fourteen:

1. accidents
2. cancer

3. problems from birth
4. homicide (murder)
5. pneumonia and the flu
6. heart disease
7. meningitis (an inflammation of the membranes surrounding the brain or spinal cord, usually caused by a bacterial infection)
8. suicide
9. cardiovascular diseases (diseases of the heart, veins, and arteries)
10. cerebral palsy complications (causing the part of the brain that controls the muscles not to work normally; this, in turn, causes a person to lose control of some vital muscles)*

Out of 100,000 people, forty-three die as kids, ages one to fourteen, each year. This is not a very great number compared to the whole country's population, and most of these deaths are the results of accidents, while the remainder may be split into about five categories: cancer, birth problems, murder/suicide, heart diseases, and infectious illnesses.

Dr. Norman Sherry, Caleb's doctor, told us: "Children . . . do not usually die of infectious dis-

*Vaughan and McKay, *Nelson Textbook of Pediatrics*, (Philadelphia: W. B. Saunders Publishers, 1975), pp. 4–6.

eases." The kids who do are usually children in underdeveloped countries where there are not adequate sanitary systems and food protections. American children are vaccinated against many infectious diseases, and, while there are still some very scary diseases that can cause children a lot of pain, and might even kill them, these diseases are very rare.

In order to better understand kids who have fatal diseases, we took a field trip to Whole Health Associates, which is a health center for children and adults near our school. While we were there, we watched some tapes of Mr. Rogers and Phil Donahue interviewing children who had cancer, leukemia, and other life-threatening illnesses. Some of these children knew they were going to die soon, and others were unsure as to whether or not they would live. The tapes were difficult to watch but were very interesting in some ways.

All the children with life-threatening diseases felt very scared, and wondered why they had been "chosen" to get these illnesses. They felt picked on. They also felt very sad, because if they died they would be leaving the people they loved. We were impressed by the children who had become accustomed to the fact that they might die, and seemed able to continue living with a positive outlook.

Many people feel that if any child, for example, a boy, has a life-threatening illness, he should be told. It is his life and his business, and it's not fair to keep this information from him. It is best for him to find out directly from his parents. This gives him the chance to do the things he wants to do before his death. A dying child may want to talk to certain people, to tell them something secret and special.

The children on the tapes found it helpful to talk to other kids with similar diseases, because they felt supported and comforted by these children. They wanted their friends to continue being their friends, and not to be treated differently.

In addition to watching the tapes, we read some books written by children and teenagers with life-threatening illnesses. We recommend *There Is a Rainbow Behind Every Dark Cloud*, written by eleven kids between the ages of eight and nineteen at the Center for Attitudinal Healing in Tiburon, California, and published by Celestial Arts in 1978. In the foreword to the book, Gerald G. Jampolsky and Pat Taylor, two adults involved in the group, wrote,

We think healing, or "getting well," means being happy and peaceful inside. We think healing takes place when we feel nothing but love inside and when we are no longer scared or feeling bad about anything.

The children and teenagers who wrote the book had cancer, leukemia, and other possibly fatal illnesses. It is an excellent book that explains what it feels like to have a life-threatening illness, and the choices kids have in helping themselves.

Hearing the News

After we were told what our sickness was and that we might die from it, we were mad that it happened to us. The "not knowing" if we were going to get well really bothered us. Hearing that we were going to get lots of shots and lose our hair also scared us.

We did not look forward to getting X-ray therapy and chemotherapy because lots of times it made us feel worse, even though we knew it was given to us to make us well.

It was hard for most of us to talk about how we felt inside. And it was hard for us to find someone who would really listen without being afraid. Sometimes the questions we were afraid to ask were: "Am I going to die?" "What is dying like?"

We knew certain questions would bring tears to our parents' eyes so we learned not to ask those questions. All of us seemed to want to protect our parents.

At the same time, we wanted to be physically close to our parents most of the time. Lots of times we didn't want them out of our sight.

The nurses were great at the hospital. They made us feel comfortable, but we all wanted to go home.

Going Back to School

Most of us had two feelings at the same time: wanting to go back to school and being scared of going back.

It was really tough going back to school when you didn't have any hair. All the kids asked us, "What hap-

pened?" "Where's all your hair?" "Why are you wearing
that hat or that wig?"

Sometimes we met some guy who acted like a jerk
and tried to pull our hat off. Sometimes we ended up
fighting.

We didn't like feeling different. We also felt dumb
because we missed so much school and we thought we
would never catch up.

We were also mad because we missed out on sports.

The kids kept asking us what was wrong with us and
lots of times we didn't know what to say. So lots of times
we didn't say anything. We didn't feel like talking about
it.

Things You Can Do About Your Feelings

First of all, you can choose to help yourself by speak-
ing up and saying anything that is on your mind. Hiding
your feelings just makes you more scared. So don't hide
the way you feel. Just be yourself. Don't fight your angry
feelings. Just accept them and then they can quickly go
away.

It's okay to cry. It's okay not to like hospitals and shots,
to be homesick, to be upset about being lonely, and to
be mad that this is happening to you.

It's okay to feel sorry for yourself and to be mad at
the world and everyone in it. And it's okay to talk about
death and your fears about it.

We found it helpful to find other kids who have similar problems and to meet with them. We have found
that, as we helped each other, we have helped ourselves.
We have fun and don't think about being afraid.

It is helpful to find you are not alone, and that there
are other kids just like you who are going through the

same thing. Other kids have the same feelings you do about losing their hair. Kids can be more helpful than adults because they talk your language. Kids can also understand without your having to use words.

When other kids tease you, you can pay no attention to them; you can fight them; or you can choose to see that they are scared. (We found that sometimes a kid teases you because they are the ones who are scared.)

Talking About Death Can Help

We all found it helpful to talk about death. It seemed easier to talk about being afraid of dying with other kids than to talk about it with adults. Lots of times adults get nervous, change the subject, and tell us that we shouldn't think of things like that.

Drawing pictures about what we thought death was like and talking about the pictures with each other made it less scary to talk about.

It was helpful to find out how other kids looked at death.

One of us thought, "When you die, your body leaves you and your soul goes to heaven. There it joins other souls and becomes one soul. And sometimes the soul comes back to earth and acts as a guardian angel to someone." We all seemed to like that way of looking at death.

Another book written at the Center for Attitudinal Healing was written by children who have brothers and sisters with a life-threatening illness. To see a sibling dealing with a serious disease is a scary and confusing experience. These kids got together to help themselves with all the feelings — the pain, anger, jealousy, confusion, sadness. We think this book gives the reader an idea of the exact feelings some kids experience in this situation. It's called *Straight from the Siblings: Another Look at the Rainbow* and it was edited by Gloria Murray and Gerald G. Jampolsky, M.D.

"I was only six years old and my younger sister had a stroke and her kidneys failed. I found out by listening to my parents' conversations because I was afraid to ask what had happened to her. I was fairly scared. . . . I cried a lot after that. I was worried and I kept my feelings to myself. . . . My stomach was always in a knot. I tried to take life one day at a time but it really hurt. I had to learn a lot of things on my own. When I was upset I said to myself, 'You've got to figure out what to do to stop this pain. . . .' " — Heather Harris, age 11

"My mom took me back in a room and told me that my brother Keith had cancer and he might die. I asked her where did it come from. She said if they had known they might have been able to stop it.

"I asked her why did he get it and not someone else. And then I started to cry and I felt like dying." — Kurth Miller, age 13

"Well, here I am. Wondering what I am doing, why I am sitting here on the sixth floor of the hospital. Afraid and scared about what is going on. All they have told me is that my little sister is very sick and has some sort of disease.

"After a few minutes I went into a conference room. In there were my parents, the doctor and my sister. My little sister was looking so different. She looked skinny and pale. Oh what a change from my bright and happy sister! My mother looked weepy and my father upset. My sister had leukemia, a form of cancer that is life-threatening. My sister might die. The thought came to me like a punch in the stomach. I finally caught on. It was so scary! Why did my sister get this? Why not me? I was so confused inside I didn't know what to do, so I cried." — Amy Dezendorf, age 14

"William's hair came out so gradually that I didn't really notice. But other people did, especially my friends. On my birthday I had some friends spend the night. In the morning William was eating breakfast with us. I noticed all my friends were quiet, which was unusual for them. When we went downstairs after breakfast to get dressed, they all started swarming around me, asking questions. 'What happened to your brother?' Or, 'Why is your brother bald?' I realized that none of my friends had been prepared, so it must have been quite a shock. It would probably be a good idea to let people know what they're in for. I feared that William would die, and because all my brothers and sisters had moved, I would be like an *only child*.

"My advice is that doctors and parents ought to give information to the *brothers and sisters straight!* Sometimes, instead of telling them the truth, parents and doctors tell siblings a lot of baloney. It is easier to handle when you at least have all the facts." — Maria Stein, age 15

* * *

"When my sister was in the hospital with leukemia my mother gave all her attention to her and she was hardly ever home. And my sister got extra presents. I almost wished I could be sick, too." — Nathaniel Fennell, age 10

"On August 15th, 1980, my little brother died of a stroke. He had a blood clot in his neck because of too much radiation. His death was a real shock to me and I was very scared. I was afraid of what the rest of my life would be like without him. As time moved on, the thought of his death wasn't so bad anymore because I started to live my life. I started to feel better.

"I think the best way is to get your mind off of it. I was invited to go fishing. I had a good time. When I came home I felt upset again but realized that when I had a fun time I didn't feel sad." — Steven Bird, age 13

Regardless of how much support a child has, when he or she has a life-threatening illness, facing the fact that he or she might die is a difficult and frightening experience. For many kids, this is a situation they never have to deal with, because they will live to be adults, and they will grow into a broader understanding of death and dying. However, for these special children who confront serious illnesses, a lot of love, support, and information can help them through this difficult experience.

7

Violent Deaths

WHY WE ARE INCLUDING VIOLENT DEATHS IN THIS BOOK

A s we have seen, most people do not die from violent causes, such as suicide, murder, or accidents. Most people die of old age, cancer, and other diseases. However, we wanted to include this topic in the book, because kids are affected by all kinds of violent death.

Alex was scared once by a rumor that some people dressed like clowns were going around Cambridge and murdering kids. A couple of his friends said they knew some other kids who were chased by the clowns and almost caught. At first he believed them, but then he read in the newspaper that it was a big hoax. He then felt relieved.

Caleb had an experience with a bunch of older kids when he was six. One day, when he was riding his bike, a gang stopped him on the road. He managed to escape, but as he ran away, they said they were going to look him up in the phone book and "get him." Luckily, they never did. At first Caleb was scared, but he finally got over it.

When Kate was in nursery school, her teacher read the class an article about a boy being kidnapped after accepting a ride from a stranger. When she came home from school, Kate was afraid to go into her backyard or on the street by herself. She was afraid that someone would crawl through her window and kidnap her. This never happened, but she was scared for two years.

While most of us haven't had any experiences with violent deaths, we all have a lot of fears due to stories we've heard. Some kids, however, do find themselves in situations where they have to deal with actual violent deaths, due to accidents, murders, or suicides. These are often even more frightening than the rumors and stories we've heard.

ACCIDENTS

Accidental deaths are among the most shocking kinds, because they happen without any notice. They are almost totally out of anyone's control and are always surprises.

Jorie's mother died in an accident caused by a tornado. Jorie and her family were completely shocked, because it happened so suddenly. Jorie said that her father took it very hard and "numbed out" for a little while. Jorie also told us that she has had fantasies about saving her mother.

Some common accidents that kill people are: car accidents, plane accidents, drowning, fires, and falling off high places.

To prevent getting into an accident of any kind, it's important for kids to do their best to follow safety precautions. Common sense should be used at all times, and kids should pay particular attention when they are around dangerous items — stoves, subway tracks, knives. Sometimes kids enjoy playing around with danger, and daring one another to take certain kinds of risks. As much as this can be playful and challenging, it is unwise to let his get out of control.

In case you or someone you are with is involved in an accident, there are some things you should know. Be ready to get help by dialing the police or fire department on the telephone, or by running for assistance to a person with medical training. It is also helpful if kids are aware of basic first-aid techniques, and are able to deal with medical problems that arise when no other help is available. Since you can never predict when accidents will happen, it's important to be able to respond to these situations with calmness and skill, even if they are frightening to you.

SUICIDE

Suicide is one of the most tragic kinds of death, because it is like throwing away your life for no good cause. Some of the reasons young people kill themselves are because they are deeply depressed, they are not given a chance in life, they feel unloved and alone, or they have suffered a painful loss of a friend or family member. A suicidal person feels that life is too difficult, and there is no reason to continue living. Some young people commit suicide slowly, through the abuse of drugs and alcohol. Others kill themselves quickly — by hanging or shooting themselves, for example.

If someone you know feels suicidal, have him or her seek professional help. They should talk to a clergy person, psychiatrist, or counselor. There are also hotlines in most cities (like the Samaritans in Boston) that are staffed by trained counselors who can help them feel better.

MURDER

Murder tends to scare kids more than anything else, because it makes them feel defenseless and vulnerable.

One girl we talked with found her mother murdered. The murder took place at night while the girl was asleep, and when she walked into her mother's room in the morning, she found her mother lying dead on the bed. Her mother had been badly stabbed.

The girl immediately called the police, her older sister, and some friends. The police took care of her mother's body, and the girl went to a friend's house. The mother's boyfriend had been drunk the night of the murder. They had gotten into an argument, and he killed her. The girl had liked him before this happened, but now she feels a lot of hatred for him. He is in jail now for twenty years.

When we talked to the girl, she told us that she used to feel suicidal and had dreams about the murder, but now she says that she is getting over her mother's death.

ASSASSINATIONS

An assassination is the murder of a politician or other important public figure. Some of the famous people who have been assassinated during the last few decades include President John F. Kennedy, Martin Luther King, Jr., and rock star John Lennon.

The assassination of a president or other political figure has far-reaching consequences. An entire nation can be completely paralyzed by the loss of a leader, and sometimes, as when President Kennedy was killed, the entire world mourns. This kind of a sudden and tragic loss triggers strong emotional reactions — shock, rage, and sadness — as seen in the 1968 assassination of Martin Luther King, Jr. Many of the followers of this civil rights leader became so enraged and frustrated that they rioted in the streets and burned buildings in protest. It was so unfair that a man who stood for peace was shot in the prime of his life.

A celebrity's murder can be just as traumatic. One musician whose death affected many, many people was former Beatle John Lennon. Lennon was shot outside his New York apartment on December 9, 1980. As the news spread, America and the world went into shock and experienced great sorrow at the loss of this artist. He was somebody who had made us laugh, and who had taught many young people to feel. By murdering him, the killer had murdered a song.

The assassination or other violent death of a famous person can come as quite a shock to kids. Often this is one of the first experiences a child has with the death of another human being, and even if he or she hasn't personally known the celebrity, the death may cause strong feelings of shock, sadness, and loss in the child. The celebrity may have served as one of the child's role models, and he or she might feel that an important part of life has been taken away. Then, too, violence scares us. Also, sometimes we think of these celebrities as superhuman — we make them into beings greater than mortal humans — and when they die or get killed, we realize for the first time that they are, in fact, just like the rest of us.

Because celebrities play such an important role in all of our lives, their deaths — especially violent ones — leave us very upset. People should try not to dwell on the death, and instead try to remember what the celebrity was like, and how he or she changed the world for the better.

We have talked a lot about different ways that people die, and we have seen that some ways of dying are better than others. For example, dying from health problems brought on by old age is better than getting killed in a war. To help us understand our various feelings surrounding different kinds of deaths, we put together a list of fourteen common causes of death, and then put them into an order from "best to worst." This process allowed each of us in the class to understand some of our ideas about what is a "good way" to die.

We felt that the best ways to die were dying in one's sleep, of old age, and from a disease. The worst ways were from drowning, suicide, starvation, war, and a gun-shot wound. Cancer, lung disease, and car accidents were in the middle. The very worst way was to be murdered.

Then we talked about why we thought our list

turned out this way. We decided that we would all prefer to die with a minimum of pain and in a peaceful way. We felt that dying from any kind of violence takes the dignity out of death. While this "rating" of deaths may sound like a strange exercise, we found it interesting and helpful to our understanding of death and dying.

All deaths are sad, and when death comes in a violent manner — through suicide, murder, or accidents — it can seem particularly tragic. On the other hand, while no one is absolutely sure about what happens when people die, some of us believe that people experience something better and more peaceful after death.

8

Is There Life After Death?

WHAT is it like to be dead? Is it peaceful? Or is it terrifying? What happens after you die? Do you lie in the ground and rot? Do you live again?

Up to this point, this book has been about things that we are sure about — our feelings, experiences, and attitudes about death and dying. This section is about something we are not at all sure about — whether there is life after death. No one knows the answer to this question, but everyone has an opinion or belief about it. Some people think that ideas such as reincarnation or ghosts are silly, childish fantasies, but it is important to discuss these beliefs, because they are shared by so many of us.

People have many different ideas about what happens to us after we die. Some people believe that life moves along a simple line. You are born, you go through life, and you die. Then it's all over. Other people believe that life runs in a circular pattern. You are born, you go through life, you die, and then you are born again. They believe that this can happen over and over. The process of dying and then being born again is called *reincarnation*.

Another belief is that after death we go to heaven or hell, depending on whether we have been good or bad. Still others believe that they will become a ghost or spirit that wanders the earth. There is really no way to be sure what *does* happen after death.

There have been some rare cases in which a person who came close to dying believed that he or she got a glimpse of what death was like. We read a book called *Life After Life* that describes this kind of experience: "A lady who was resuscitated after a heart attack remarked: 'I began to experience the most wonderful feelings. I couldn't feel a thing in the world except peace, comfort, ease — just quietness. I felt that all my troubles were gone, and I thought to myself, well, how quiet and peaceful, and I don't hurt at all.' " Stories like this one make death sound appealing, but they have to be taken with a grain of salt, because the people reporting them didn't actually die. In the absence of any real information, we can only wonder about different possibilities.

Many people believe in the existence of heaven and hell. They picture heaven as a place very far up in the sky, where good people go when they die. People usually associate heaven with the color white, as well as with wings and angels and sweet music. Hell is usually thought of as a hot and fiery place deep down in the earth, where everyone suffers constantly, and the devil sits waiting to throw evil people into a big pot full of boiling red liquid!

Lisa Marlin, a teacher in our school, thinks that there is a goal that everyone is expected to try to reach in his or her lifetime. She calls it "The Perfect Love." If you do something wrong, or didn't learn something important during a lifetime, you are forced to repeat life on earth until you learn that particular lesson. For example, if you happen to be a cat, and you catch and eat a mouse, you might have to live your next lifetime as a mouse, in order to learn you shouldn't have eaten one.

Lisa had an experience that strengthened her belief in reincarnation. One day in meditation she fell into a very deep state and began to go far back in time. Lisa told us: "I could remember having an entire past lifetime!" She remembered her life as an American Indian, when she was a teacher of meditation. This was very interesting, because meditation is one of the subjects she teaches in our school.

Pat Sargent, a parent at Fayerweather, also believes in reincarnation. We asked her if she thought it would be possible to come back after death in the form of a plant, cat, or any object. She said that you have to come back as something that is alive. What you return as depends on the particular task that you are expected to achieve in your new lifetime — if it is necessary to be a dog in order to learn a certain lesson, or to complete a certain task, you will come back as a dog. Zen Buddhists call this concept a "kharmic wheel."

Earlier in this book, we asked doctors when they consider a person dead. Lisa Marlin has a different answer. She told us: "I think when a person's soul leaves their body, and while the soul is out, the heart stops beating or they stop breathing, then they are officially dead."

Some people believe that we have a spiritual body as well as a physical body. They feel that while the physical body decomposes in the ground, the spiritual body goes somewhere else.

Lisa believes that the soul is separate from the body, and she claims that she has had what's called an "out-of-body experience." She actually floated out of her body and could see the earth and clouds below her. As she started to float back into her body, she could see herself down on the ground, meditating.

Lisa says that an out-of-body experience prepares you for what happens to you when you die.

Pat Sargent says that out-of-body experiences are trips the spiritual body takes to teach you important lessons. Pat's mother had an out-of-body experience while she was dying. She returned to consciousness before she died with the message: "Nobody deserves the beauty of death."

Some people believe that when your soul leaves your physical body, it is reborn again in another energy form, such as another human being. They think of ghosts as souls that for some reason couldn't be reborn into another energy form.

It's clear to us that people have many different ideas about what happens to a person after death. While some of these ideas may seem a little strange, we think it's important at least to consider the possibilities, since none of us can know for certain what is going to take place after we die. It is comforting to believe that something more than simply lying in the ground happens after death.

❧ 9 ❧

What We Have Learned

OUR year-long work on this book affected us in
many ways. We examined a lot of the issues
surrounding death and dying in American society,
and we became aware of the many diverse feelings
people have on this subject. We also learned that a
lot of the mystery and fear surrounding death has
been brought about by ignorance and avoidance,
and, the more we learned throughout the year, the
more comfortable we became with this difficult subject.

Many of us now think about death in a broader
way than we had previously, and we realize now
that death is a very complex topic. Billy has found
that he understands many of the issues surrounding
death a lot better than before we worked on the
book, and he is, in fact, more interested in the subject now than he was before. Billy also feels that in
the future, when a relative dies, he won't be as con-

fused about it. Caleb, too, feels that a lot of the mystery surrounding the topic has been removed for him. By coming to terms with death and learning to accept it as a part of the life cycle, we feel we can lead happier and more productive lives.

Perhaps the most important thing we have learned is that children can be helpful to people who are dying. We hope that others reading this book will also benefit from this information, and find a way to aid people they know who may have a terminal illness. We also hope this book will make children less afraid of dealing with a dying person, and take some of the mystery and strangeness out of this human situation.

It is difficult for anyone to tell a person that he or she is dying, but it is important for people to be told this information directly and honestly, rather than to learn about it through an unfortunate slip. The doctor (or the friend or family member) who knows should say something like, "You have a serious illness for which, right now, there is no cure. This disease usually causes death." Then the doctor should answer any questions, telling the truth to the best of his or her ability. He or she should be honest, but leave *some* room for hope.

When a person is told that they are dying, they may not hear correctly at first, because it hurts too much to face this painful fact. As they go on, day by day, they will accept a little more of the truth and understand a little more about their sickness.

According to well-known Swedish doctor Eliza-beth Kubler-Ross, there are five stages a person goes through when they learn of their impending death. The first stage involves denial and isolation. When people are first told that they are terminally ill, it is so painful that their immediate reaction is — not me! This couldn't happen to me!

After a while, their mood changes, and they slowly begin to face the fact that they are dying. Then they enter the second stage — anger. People become angry when they realize that they are dying: "Why me? What brought this on? What does this have to do with me?"

Stage three involves bargaining. The person was sad at first, then angry, but now is their time to be "good." People think that if they cooperate, then maybe they will be better off.

Stage four is depression. At this time the patient no longer denies his or her condition — they feel a great sense of loss, and helplessness.

Stage five is the final acceptance of the fact that they are dying, that they can't fight it or deny it any longer. The anger and pain is replaced by peaceful-ness. They are ready to die in a calm, accepting way.

Being aware of these stages of reaction can help us relate to the feelings of the dying and understand them better. We recommend that more children receive some kind of education about death and dying, through school, through their family, or through a church or synagogue. It is valuable for kids to share their feelings with one another, and not to be pressured into thinking they should feel a certain way. It is important to explain facts about death and dying to kids, because ignorance fosters fear.

It is also important for adults to become more comfortable with the subject of death and dying. As long as adults remain afraid of death, they will continue to influence children with their unhealthy and negative feelings. We hope that children can lead the way in dealing with death and dying with a healthier and happier approach, and we look forward to the time when all people will better understand and accept the cycle of life and death, so that they will be able to live richer and more satisfying lives.

Other Books About Death and Dying

There are many books for children and teen-agers about death and dying — both fiction and nonfiction. These books were very good and helpful to us:

A TASTE OF BLACKBERRIES
By Doris Buchanan Smith
New York: Thomas Y. Crowell, 1973

This book is about a boy who dies and how his best friend deals with it. It is written from his friend's point-of-view. It is good for giving another child's point-of-view and experience with death, but it was kind of sad, and Jamey felt very sorry for the friend. It is very easy reading and useful for younger children.

HOW DOES IT FEEL WHEN A PARENT DIES?
By Jill Krementz
New York: Alfred A. Knopf, 1981

This book is about eighteen kids, each of whom has experienced the death of a mother or father. It describes how each child felt, how the remaining parent felt, and the funeral services that took place. It includes touching photographs of each child.

Any child reading this book would see how painful and horrible it would be to find one of your parents dead. The reader would also learn about the kind of treatment these children received from school and neighborhood friends, and how these relationships may change when a parent dies. Most impressive, however, is the amount of strength that every child in this book seems to have.

Macy had mixed feelings about the book. She didn't feel happy about what happened to these kids, but the writing was fresh and down-to-earth, so she couldn't help but like the book. Every child who has lost a parent should read it, and if the child is under nine, someone should read it to him or her.

CHARLOTTE'S WEB
By E. B. White
New York: Harper & Row, 1952

This book is about a friendship between Wilbur, a pig, and Charlotte, a spider, and how Charlotte saves Wilbur's life, and how Wilbur learns that friendship is important to him. Charlotte lives a good life and helps others, and is able to talk about her dying and knows that the things she leaves behind will be well cared for. This makes her feel better about her dying.

Tanya's favorite part was when Charlotte told Wilbur that she was going to die. It was sad, and Wilbur's reactions were emotional and realistic. The book makes you realize how important having a good friend is. Tanya recommends it to almost everyone.

WHOSE LIFE IS IT ANYWAY?
By Brian Clark
New York: Avon Books, 1978

A sculptor is paralyzed from the neck down when he is in a road accident, and a broken rib cuts through his spinal column. He comes to the conclusion that he is useless and wants to die, but the doctors won't let him. The book follows him from his decision to die because he is totally dependent on machines and other people, to the court trial about whether he should be allowed to die. John recommends this book to kids who are interested in the ethics of euthanasia and are age ten and older. The book made him both happy and sad.

THERE ARE TWO KINDS OF TERRIBLE
By Peggy Mann
New York: Doubleday & Co., Inc., 1977

This book is about a child whose mother died from cancer. The boy is not very close to his father at first, but by the end of the book they get a lot closer. This story would be very helpful to a child if his or her parent was dying. One part that Kama liked very much was the scene in which the mother died. This was very sad, but by the end of the book, Kama felt good. We recommend the book to readers above the age of ten.

THAT'S WHAT FRIENDS ARE FOR
By Ronald Kidd
Nashville: Thomas Nelson, Inc., 1978

The book is about two seventh-graders — Gary Matthews and Scott Lewis. Gary accidentally finds out that Scott has a fatal disease, and since Scott doesn't want anyone to know, Gary has to keep this bottled up inside him. The book deals more with friendship than death and dying, but Seth found that it taught him a lot about this kind of friendship.

THE CALL OF THE WILD
By Jack London
New York: Macmillan, Inc., 1970. (Originally published 1903.)

Caleb reviewed this book and thought that it was good, and it made him feel both interested and sad. It tells the life of Buck, a dog who lives in a suburb of California and is suddenly sold to an Alaskan sled driver. He lives with the sled driver and works for a long time, and then is passed from master to master. Buck learns to survive the savagery of the life of Klondike sled dogs, and finally decides to retire with a wolf pack in a faraway forest. The book presents a very interesting view of death from the perspective of an animal.

TIGER EYES
By Judy Blume
Scarsdale, NY: Bradbury Press, 1981

Macy and Alex both read this book and thought it was an excellent book for kids above the age of eleven. The book is about Davey Wexler and her brother and mother, and how they deal with the murder of their father. Blume does a good job writing of Davey's paranoid feelings after her father gets killed. A kid can learn much from this book, particularly about dealing with an abrupt death and how family members (especially mothers) may react. It does a good job of covering friends and classmate reactions, and includes getting help from a psychiatrist. It is very helpful in dealing with murders and other violent deaths.